FRESHLY PICKED

Caitlin Press Inc.
8100 Alderwood Road, Halfmoon Bay, BC V0N 1Y1
www.caitlin-press.com
Text and cover design by Vici Johnstone

Printed in Canada

Caitlin Press Inc. acknowledges financial support from the Government of Canada and the Canada Council for the Arts, and the Province of British Columbia through the British Columbia Arts Council and the Book Publisher's Tax Credit.

Library and Archives Canada Cataloguing in Publication

Reid, Jane, author
    Freshly picked : a locavore's love affair with BC's bounty / Jane Reid.

ISBN 978-1-987915-79-2 (softcover)
    1. Local foods—British Columbia. 2. Food industry and trade—British Columbia. 3. Farm produce—British Columbia.
I. Title.

TX360.C32B747 2018   641.3009711   C2018-903397-5

FRESHLY PICKED

A Locavore's
Love Affair with
BC's Bounty

Jane Reid

CAITLIN PRESS

This book is dedicated to the farmers of British Columbia.

CONTENTS

Legend

1 — Fraser Valley
2 — Saanich Peninsula
   and Metchosin
3 — Cowichan Valley
4 — Comox Valley
5 — Pemberton Valley
6 — Sunshine Coast
7 — Southern Gulf Islands
8 — Bulkley Valley
9 — Peace River District
10 — Robson Valley
11 — Cariboo
12   Lower Thompson/Lillooet
13 — Similkameen
14 — Okanagan Valley
15 — Slocan Valley (Kootenays)
16 — Creston Valley (Kootenays)
17 — Bella Coola Valley
18 — Lower Skeena

FARMING AREAS IN BC

- Atlin

Fort St. John
⑨ •
Dawson Creek •

Prince Rupert •

⑱ •Smithers
Terrace ⑧
•Burns Lake
Vanderhoof •
•Prince George

McBride •
Quesnel • ⑩

Bella Coola• ⑰
⑪
• Williams Lake

Lillooet •
Salmon Arm

Whistler • Kamloops
⑤
⑫

Courtenay/Comox
⑭ •Kelowna
⑥ Nelson •
⑯
Vancouver
④ ⑬ ⑮ •Creston
Vancouver Island
① Keremeos
UNITED STATES
③ ⑦
Victoria ⑦ ② Southern Gulf Islands

Fruit and Vegetable Availabilty Charts

	Legend
▓ (shaded)	Available Fresh
■	Greenhouse Grown
◈	Stored

Vegetables	J	F	M	A	M	J	J	A	S	O	N	D
Artichokes	◈	◈	◈	◈	◈	◈	◈	▓	▓	▓	◈	◈
Asparagus				▓	▓							
Beans – Green							▓	▓	▓	▓		
Beets	◈	◈	◈	◈	◈	▓	▓	▓	▓	▓	▓	◈
Broccoli						▓	▓	▓	▓	▓	▓	
Brussels Sprouts								▓	▓	▓	▓	▓
Cabbage – Green	◈	◈	◈			▓	▓	▓	▓	▓	▓	◈
Cabbage — Savoy & Red	◈	◈	◈				▓	▓	▓	▓	▓	◈
Carrots	◈	◈				▓	▓	▓	▓	▓	▓	◈
Cauliflower						▓	▓	▓	▓	▓	▓	
Celery						▓	▓	▓	▓	▓	▓	
Chard – Swiss					▓	▓	▓	▓	▓	▓	▓	
Corn						▓	▓	▓	▓			
Cucumbers		■	■	■	■	■	■	■	■	■	■	
Fennel (Bulb)						▓	▓	▓	▓	▓		

Vegetables	J	F	M	A	M	J	J	A	S	O	N	D
Garlic	◆	◆	◆	◆	◆	◆	◆	◆	◆	◆	◆	◆
Kale	▓	▓	▓	▓	▓	▓	▓	▓	▓	▓	▓	▓
Leeks	▓	▓	▓				▓	▓	▓	▓	▓	▓
Lettuce	■	■	■	■	■	■	■	■	■	■	■	■
Mushrooms*	▓	▓	▓	▓	▓	▓	▓	▓	▓	▓	▓	▓
Mustard Greens					▓	▓	▓	▓	▓			
Onions – Green					▓	▓	▓	▓	▓			
Onions – Red & Yellow	◆	◆	◆	◆	◆	◆	◆	◆	◆	◆	◆	◆
Parsnips	◆	◆	◆				▓	▓	▓	▓		◆
Peas						▓	▓					
Peppers			■	■	■	■	■	■	■	■	■	
Potatoes – New					▓	▓	▓					
Potatoes – Red, Russet & Yellow	◆	◆	◆	◆	◆			▓	▓	▓		◆
Potatoes – White	◆	◆	◆					▓	▓			◆
Pumpkin									▓	▓	▓	◆
Radishes				▓	▓	▓	▓	▓				
Rhubarb – Field				▓	▓	▓						
Rutabagas	◆	◆	◆	◆				▓	▓	▓		◆
Salad Greens				▓	▓	▓	▓	▓	▓			
Shallots	◆	◆	◆	◆				▓	◆	◆	◆	◆

Vegetables	J	F	M	A	M	J	J	A	S	O	N	D
Spinach				▒	▒	▒	▒	▒	▒	▒		
Squash – Summer						▒	▒	▒	▒			
Squash – Winter	◈	◈	◈						▒	▒	▒	◈
Tomatoes					■	■	■	■	■	■	■	■
Turnips – White	◈	◈	◈			▒	▒	▒	▒	▒		◈
Zucchini						▒	▒	▒	▒	▒		

* Commercially grown.

Availability in the above chart is for vegetables grown in Southwestern BC (Lower Mainland) and Southern Vancouver Island. For vegetables grown farther north, availability may be delayed by a week or two.

Chart compiled with data provided by Farm Folk City Folk.

Fruit	J	F	M	A	M	J	J	A	S	O	N	D
Apples	◆	◆	◆	◆	◆			■	■	■	◆	◆
Apricots							■					
Blackberries								■	■			
Blueberries							■	■	■			
Cherries						■	■					
Cranberries									■	■		
Currants							■					
Grapes									■	■		
Melons								■	■			
Nectarines								■				
Peaches								■	■			
Pears	◆	◆	◆						■	◆	◆	◆
Plums									■			
Raspberries							■	■				
Rhubarb				■	■	■	■					
Strawberries						■	■					

If the spring has been unusually warm and sunny, fruits may ripen a week or two earlier than normal. Likewise, cold, rainy weather may delay the start of the season.

Fruits ripen earliest in the southern parts of BC, such as the Southern Okanagan. Fruits may take another week or two to ripen in the Northern Okanagan and farther north.

New varieties of fruits are constantly being researched and tested with the aim of extending the regular season. When successful, new varieties mean fresh BC fruits can be enjoyed over a longer period.

ACKNOWLEDGEMENTS

This book is in your hands because I had help along the way—and lots of it. First and foremost, I am grateful to Zsuzsi Gartner, mentor and friend, who over time has taught and encouraged me, edited my words, and suggested a way forward. *Freshly Picked* would not have been written without her. Sincere thanks go to Debbra Mikaelsen of *Edible Vancouver &Wine Country* magazine, who originally published and edited my pieces. Her kind words made such a difference. Thanks also to editor AnnMarie MacKinnon, who continued her support.

I am deeply indebted to Stella Harvey, founder of the Whistler Writers Festival, for her advice and the opportunities provided for writers through her efforts with the Whistler Writing Society, including my first contact with Vici Johnstone of Caitlin Press. I owe Vici immense thanks for believing in this book right from the start and seeing it through from beginning to end. Thank you also to the Caitlin Press team of Holly Vestad and Michael Despotovic plus Meg Yamamoto, Patricia Wolfe and Christine Savage.

I am blessed to have been involved with two writing critique groups over the past ten years, and I treasure the input and friendship that has improved my writing along the way. Heartfelt thanks and love to Penny, Brigitte, Rachael, Shannon, Karen, Claire, Suzanne, Ali, Anya, Yulia and Diane.

To the farmers, growers and distributors who have helped me understand what they do and to all those who have shared recipes and photos, thank you. In particular, I am grateful to the farmers of the beautiful Pemberton Valley, whose hard work, unbridled enthusiasm and love of the land are a constant inspiration.

Lastly, I am ever grateful to my family for reading chapter after chapter—my sister, Darcy, for her unequalled, enthusiastic support, my daughters, Sally and Maddie, for their welcome contributions, and my husband Rick, my biggest, most loyal fan as well as my life partner, for his valuable insights and endless patience.

Nothing matches the taste of freshly picked fruits and vegetables in season, grown in BC on the family farm. Photo: Michelle Headly for Laughing Crow Organics, Pemberton, BC.

When inspired by the extraordinary taste of locally grown harvests, you may find yourself falling in love all over again with fruits and vegetables you have known all your life. Photo: Teri Virbickis/Shutterstock.com

INTRODUCTION

What is more agreeable than gathering to enjoy a tasty, satisfying meal with family and friends? I learned the answer to that question when I was young and lived in Quebec—la Belle Province *avec la différence*. It was there that I came to appreciate food well prepared and savoured with celebratory reverence. Eating can't always be an occasion, but I happily subscribe to the tenet that, whenever possible, we should live to eat, not eat to live.

The second part of my alimentary education came about when my family moved across the country to British Columbia. Lotus Land, we called it back then. Having lived only in wild places distant from any agriculture, it was soon apparent to me that BC was special. With one delightful, delicious encounter after another—such as grabbling for baby potatoes in a Ladner field—I made an acquaintance with the diverse and plentiful bounty that is grown in this province. It was a new and wonderful taste experience for me, and I relished the just picked, the newly dug and the recently reaped like a religious convert (or a Quebec chef).

The magic of the ever-changing offerings of the land became part of the charm and the challenge for me. "Get it before it's gone" turned into my mantra—as in, Is raspberry season finished already? The hunt was always on—not for a good deal at the mall but for the best and the freshest BC fruits and vegetables. The reward was flavour, one delectable mouthful after another as the growing season rolled by.

My enthusiasm for fresh local food remains undimmed. In this day of threatened agricultural land and climate change, my ardour has only increased. When produce sections remain almost unchanged twelve months of the year, it is easy to lose the connection to our land, our farmers and the plants that feed us. Yet it is a connection that many of us crave. It's why we meander through farmers' markets, plant vegetable gardens, check out roadside stands and venture into the U-pick berry patch. Given the choice, I think we prefer to know where our food comes from, we like it to be fresh and local, and we believe in supporting our farmers and saving our farmland. Buying locally grown produce just seems like the right thing to do, even if it means digging a little deeper and learning a little more.

As with almost everything, a bit of knowledge goes a long way. Finding local bounty is easier when we know what grows when and where, and what can be stored. When will we see local peaches at the market? What local crops can we eat all winter? How do we tell a local from a tourist in the grocery store? How do we find the best and the freshest? The answers can be found inside these pages.

To make it easy, chapters are arranged by season, highlighting one fruit and vegetable after another from upstart spring radishes to autumn dawdlers like acorn squash. Selected chapters have already made an appearance in *Edible Vancouver & Wine Country* magazine. Availability charts sum up the timeline of BC's harvests, making it easy to know what to look for in June, or in October.

My love affair with BC's fruits and vegetables grew as I discovered they have quirky histories and peculiar growing habits all their own—like the fascinating sex life of corn or the checkered reputation of garlic. These stories, along with tales of my very personal relationships with BC's edible offerings—such as when I first met a green bean that wasn't out of a can—make their way into these pages as well.

And then there is the final and most important part—the eating! I share recipes and insights to bring out the best flavour at the dinner table, or to preserve the taste of summer sunshine for winter enjoyment: how to store a watermelon, whip up jewel-like cranberry sauce or freeze piquant roasted cherry tomatoes. When inspired by locally grown foods, you may find yourself falling in love all over again with the fruits and vegetables you have known all your life. Taste rules—and there is nothing better than sitting down at the table to relish and celebrate the marvellous diversity and flavour of BC's bounty.

Opposite: Blackberries grow with wild abandon in many parts of British Columbia, lining roadsides, fields and fences—offering a delicious, though prickly, harvest free for the picking every summer. Photo:iStock.com/Hillview1

SPRING

LONG LIVE SPARGELZEIT!
AN ODE TO ASPARAGUS

The ancient Romans loved it. Andy Warhol painted it. And there is a museum in Germany solely dedicated to it. I am referring to asparagus, that most strange and marvellous vegetable.

One spring a few years ago, my husband and I spent an idyllic week in Prad, a charming village in the Italian Alps. Being next door to Austria, it's an appealing mix of Germanic tidiness and efficiency married with Italian flair. And food from both traditions; how good is that? On our first night, we wandered down to a restaurant. Inserted in the menu was a full page of specials, every one of them featuring asparagus. We had arrived smack in the middle of Spargelzeit, or asparagus season—cause for celebration.

Asparagus is an old soul. Four thousand years ago, people in the Middle East and Egypt gathered and ate wild asparagus. Two thousand years later, the Romans were the first to cultivate the plant we know today, harvesting it every spring. So enamoured were the ancient Romans with asparagus that swift runners and chariots were sent to the Alps to freeze a supply for later feasting. Special ships—the "asparagus fleet"—transported the vegetable quickly to asparagusless parts of the Roman Empire.

Asparagus then disappeared—like many civilized elements—for a few hundred years during the Dark Ages in Europe. It made a reappearance during the Renaissance and eventually became a darling of the monarchy. Louis XIV, ever self-indulgent, had greenhouses specially built in France to grow asparagus for most of the year.

Opposite: Asparagus, an oddball in the vegetable world, emerges phoenix-like from the soil in early spring, signalling the welcome start of the growing season in BC. Photo: msgrafixx/Shutterstock.com

The vegetable, expensive for the masses, was known as the "royal vegetable."

Luckily for us, times have changed. Asparagus, more than any other vegetable (except maybe rhubarb, its seasonal partner), signals the arrival of spring. It is one of the first fresh local veggies we eat after a long winter. Of course, we can now eat asparagus almost any time of the year in our land of supermarket foods that have travelled ten thousand kilometres. Asparagus in the fall means it's spring in Peru. Asparagus in January means it's spring in Mexico. But asparagus in May means it is spring in BC.

Watch for BC-grown asparagus in markets and groceries as early as April. Get it before it's gone—usually by mid-June. Photo: Stephanie Studer/Unsplash

Asparagus farmers are found on Vancouver Island, in the Kootenays and in the Okanagan Valley. As usual, Washington production dwarfs ours, but hey, it's closer than Peru. These farmers all share a singular virtue: patience. Asparagus farming is not for the impetuous. It takes three years of waiting after planting crowns, which are the equivalent of bulbs for asparagus, before farmers can harvest the vegetable. Make that four years when starting from seed.

Asparagus spears, surely one of the oddest looking of all vegetables, start to rise phoenix-like—some would say phallic-like—from the soil in early spring. To harvest, they are cut or snapped off near the ground. It is back-breaking work, unchanged since Roman times. Machines are also used in an attempt to make things easier by allowing pickers to sit or even lie down as they roll along, low to the ground, cutting spears as they go. Harvesting continues as new spears appear, shooting from the ground in an inevitable, never-ending effort to reproduce, as with all growing things. In ideal conditions (that would be in California), the stalks can grow up to twenty-five centimetres in twenty-four hours, which surely must be some kind of vegetable record.

After six weeks or so, the stalks get spindlier, and harvesting is halted. The remaining asparagus is left to grow, and each one of the little raised triangles running up the spears opens up, sending a tall, fine and feathery stem up to 150 centimetres high to blow gently in the wind. At this stage, they look more like the ubiquitous asparagus ferns (a close, inedible relative) that lurked in almost every home in the 1970s—perched on windowsills or slung up in macramé—than the asparagus we eat.

But there's another characteristic that sets asparagus apart from most other vegetables. It has staying power. Asparagus is a perennial, which means that every year it comes back again in soil warmed by the watery spring sunshine. Unlike many other veggies, which are grown from seed, harvested, then plowed under or allowed to rot in situ, asparagus rises again, year after year after year—for up to thirty seasons. Who says that patience has no reward?

Oh, and one more thing. No other vegetable makes your pee smell. Not all of us are genetically endowed to actually detect the odour, but most of us produce it. The ancients make no mention of this characteristic, perhaps because they were assaulted with other plentiful and powerful scents. Not-so-ancient lore—during the 1800s—says that a sign posted in a British men's club read, "During asparagus season, members are requested not to relieve themselves in the hat stand."

There is an asparagus field in Pemberton, near my home in Whistler. I am fortunate, through a friend, to have access to the harvest—all of it unbelievably tender, all of it tasting like spring sprung from the ground. Washington and BC asparagus starts to show up in local stores and markets at the end of April through the middle of June. When buying, look for ends that appear freshly cut, and keep in mind that thinner stalks are not necessarily tenderer than thick ones. Wrap in damp paper towels or store in open plastic bags, and refrigerate, as asparagus starts to convert its sugar into starch at room temperature. Before cooking, snap the ends off to remove the tough parts, if necessary.

Roasting and grilling vegetables has become *de rigueur*. Asparagus is delicious this way, but with simple steaming, the flavour is full, the stalk is tender. To make a salad that celebrates spring, it's easy with (gasp!) the microwave. Line up the stalks in a glass pie pan, thickest ones on the outside, add a little water, cover and cook on high for three minutes. Check for tenderness by sticking a fork into the thickest stalks, and cook more as necessary, one minute at a time. Do not overcook. Pour off the water and immediately cool asparagus under cold running water. Drain and lay spears on a bed of greens—the freshest ones you can find—on your prettiest plate. Top with sliced mushrooms and chopped green onions—another spring green. Drizzle with reduced balsamic vinegar or your favourite oil-and-vinegar dressing, and you are done. Even royalty would approve.

Spring Is Sprung, the Greens Is Riz

When I was growing up, my mother—following her best instincts—insisted our family eat a salad every night. Once my sister and I were old enough to pitch in, it was our job to fill the wooden bowl. A chore. It meant getting the bowling-ball iceberg lettuce out of the crisper to tear off some leaves, slicing a few green onions and dicing one of those tasteless red orbs we called tomatoes. Day in, day out, we ate this salad. Dressing always came out of a bottle and was poured over our personal portion. No tossing allowed. Our family

Claytonia, a native woodland green, became known as miner's lettuce when gold-seekers ate it to ward off scurvy. Photo: Alyssa Belter, Plenty Wild Farms, Pemberton, BC

favourite was the obscenely orange French variety, though what was French about it remains a mystery. Thankfully, things have changed.

An early North American convert to a wider world of salad greens was the author E. Annie Proulx, who—long before *The Shipping News*—penned an entire book on salad fixings called *The Fine Art of Salad Gardening.* Written in 1985, when iceberg lettuce was still the norm, it is a loving tribute to growing and eating an assortment of exotic salad greens most of us had not heard of at the time. The Europeans wisely avoided the monotonous iceberg era and sensibly continued to eat a mélange of colourful leaves as they had always done. Over here, we've come to our senses and now eat a growing medley of greens, expanding our salad repertoire at the same time.

Farmers' markets, roadside stands and weekly harvest boxes are the best places to find a tempting selection of common and unusual spring greens straight out of the field. Photo: Rostovtsevayu/Shutterstock.com

We humans have eaten an astonishing variety of leaves gathered in the wild for thousands of years, adding valuable nutrients to our diets. Then we got smart and cultivated them to cut down on foraging time. Eating greens is such a basic act: pick the leaves and eat them raw—our own version of grazing like deer. When munching greens fresh and new, I can taste the earth. Our choices are boundless: sweet and juicy, tart and spicy, buttery or crisp, nutty or lemony, bitter or savoury, in a plethora of shades, patterns and shapes.

Lettuces were one of the first salad greens to be farmed by the ancients—the Romans, Greeks, Sumerians and Egyptians—who were enchanted with what they believed were the plants' tranquilizing, digestive and aphrodisiac effects. Corn salad (a.k.a. lamb's lettuce) started out in the wild, growing in cold conditions as a pesky weed in grain fields. It is cultivated by the French (who call it *mâche*) and Germans (who call it *feldsalat*) and is prized as a nutty-tasting addition to salads all winter. Claytonia, a native to West Coast woodlands, became known as miner's lettuce when it was gathered and eaten by fortune seekers on the Gold Rush Trail to avoid scurvy. I grow the wild version of my personal favourite, arugula (also known as rocket) in my garden as a fuss-free perennial. The Italians call it *rucola* and have eaten it for over 2,500 years. Most North Americans came late to mustards such as peppery Japanese mizuna and spinach-like Chinese tatsoi, ancient Asian greens that have become welcome staples in our ever-evolving multicultural salads.

When it comes to locally grown greens, spring cannot come too soon. Last year in late March, I was desperate for something new, green and tender after months of eating coleslaws. My search to satisfy my cravings took me to a Vancouver nursery to see what was on offer. A chill wind blew and dampness reigned as I milled around the outdoor plants—perfect conditions for growing greens—and there they were. I stood in a puddle all alone, happily admiring six-packs of overgrown lettuce seedlings in an appealing assortment of pale green, spotted red and burnished crimson. I bought a few, thinking, Why not? They were the same price as any cut, prewashed (three times)

Only a teasing of mild vinaigrette is needed to bring out the subtle flavour of a salad made from a selection of fresh, tender baby leaves from the garden or farm. Photo: DUSAN ZIDAR/Shutterstock.com

and past-its-prime salad mix from two thousand kilometres away. I transplanted them into sheltered patio pots at home, and within days, I could snip off a salad for two for dinner—a sneak preview of the growing season to come.

British Columbia farmers work hard to supply the spring greens we hanker for as the days lengthen. Lower Mainland and Vancouver Island growers get a jump on those in the wintry Okanagan and Pemberton Valleys. Our taste for fresh leaves means farmers are pushing boundaries by using plastic or cloth covers, sometimes in two or three layers, to protect tender plants from freezing in unheated greenhouses, hoop houses and cold frames during winter and early spring. Fall seeding means hardy plants like spinach, corn salad, kale and chard can overwinter when they're young and resilient.

In balmier areas, these plants allow non-stop harvesting so local greens show up all winter. In chillier climes, the plants rest a while, then resurrect themselves to produce harvests starting in April. Lettuces, radicchio and salad mix staples like mizuna, arugula, red mustard and tatsoi follow their hardy cousins. Soon, radishes, white hakurei turnips, green onions and chives join in the fun. Intermittent and repeated sowings under cover, then outdoors when the soil is no longer soggy, keep the harvest coming into later spring and summer.

Salad mixes are made of baby leaves, all hand-picked, the outer lettuce leaves plucked before the plant grows into a full-sized head. Other greens like the mustards are snipped when they are seven to ten centimetres tall. Not easily deterred, many regrow up to two more times and have earned the name "cut-and-come-again" greens.

Some BC growers sell salad mixes in the rigid clamshell packages found in grocery chains, but it is an expensive and regulated process. Check the fine print on the label to buy local. Most small farmers bag the crop, leaving greens unwashed or only lightly washed so they last longer in our fridges. Winter or early spring farmers' markets and CSA (community-supported agriculture) boxes are good places to find just-picked BC greens in season.

To fully savour the newest salad leaves, nothing more than a mild vinaigrette is needed. Toss greens with your favourite or mine: combine two tablespoons olive oil, one tablespoon cider vinegar, two teaspoons maple syrup and one teaspoon curry powder or Dijon mustard. For a heartier salad, top a plate of fresh greens with artfully arranged hard-boiled egg slices, sprinkle with sliced local green onions or chives and add a stream of vinaigrette. Dig in and thank BC farmers for their tireless hard work that, in spring, is only just beginning.

SPICY SPRING:
RADISHES AND GREEN ONIONS

Nothing says spring has arrived like the first radishes at the farmers' market, stacked high with their rosy roots bundled into bouquets like flowers. Green onions are often nestled beside them, bunches piled on top of one another, crisp and piquant. To complete the spring chorus, salad greens are right there too. A threesome in perfect harmony for salad eating, new and fresh, inviting us to buy and celebrate the beginning of another growing season.

Early radishes, often called spring radishes, are the sprinters of the vegetable world: a mere four to five weeks after their tiny seeds are planted, they are ready to be pulled out of the ground by their leafy green tops. Not keen on hanging around in the dirt, they must be harvested quickly; otherwise they get tired and pithy. Farmers plant seeds every one or two weeks—called succession planting— starting in March and continuing until the end of September, to keep us in radishes all summer. However, the little reds love cool soil and cool weather, so spring harvests are often best.

Green onions are a little slower off the mark, taking fifty to sixty days to grow from seed. Like radishes, they like to start off early in chilly weather. Once they grow tall enough, their drinking straw–like leaves and roots are pulled from the ground all at once, to be bundled—which is why they are sometimes called bunching onions. They are also called scallions, spring onions, Welsh onions, Japanese onions or salad onions—just to keep us on our toes.

It takes a mere four to five weeks for speedy spring radishes to grow from tiny seeds into leafy-topped spicy delights ready for eating. Photo: Markus Spiske/Unsplash

It's easy to grow your own green onions, even in a container. In spring, head to the local nursery and pass right by the seed section (tempting, I know) to ask for onion sets. These small bulbs, the size of a large garlic clove, give you a head start over seeds. Buy white or yellow onion varieties, usually available in mesh bags for next to nothing. At home, plant them close together—2.5 centimetres apart—in any sort of container filled with potting soil, with their pointy ends barely sticking up out of the soil. Put them in a sunny spot if you have it, then water and wait. Soon green tips will emerge (if they hadn't already in the store) and grow up into…green onions. You can snip them off at the base as you need them (best to leave a couple behind) and new ones will grow. This is called "cut-and-come-again" in the gardening world—a miraculous and marvellous phenomenon.

Radishes and green onions are grown and eaten around the world. Both may have originated in Asia and spread westward to be used by the Indians, Egyptians, Romans and Greeks, and eventually Europeans and North Americans. Radishes are a member of the brassica or cole family, like broccoli, kale, cabbage and mustards, which give a hint of their peppery origins. Crossbreeding and Mother Nature have given us an astonishing number of radish types of different shapes, sizes, colours and flavours. The spicy French Noir Long Maraicher with black skin and white innards and the mild Chinese Watermelon with, predictably, a pale green exterior hiding pinkish insides are just two examples of how exotic radishes can be.

In Asia, radishes really get the respect they deserve. Asian varieties, called daikon or winter radishes, take longer to grow, being much larger than smaller spring radishes. They can be planted in early spring, to be harvested at the same time as green onions, or in late summer to provide fall harvests. Daikon are often white and carrot shaped and look suspiciously like oversized parsnips. Some varieties grow into the giants of the radish world, measuring up to sixty centimetres long and ten centimetres wide and weighing up to thirty kilograms. That's some radish. When pulled out of the ground

in the autumn, daikon are pickled or stored over the winter like other root vegetables, to be used in stir-fries, soups and stews. These
roots are a mainstay favourite of Asian diets. The record holders—
the Koreans—eat thirty kilograms of them per person per year,
mostly in spicy pickled kimchi.

Radishes also play a starring role in Oaxaca, Mexico—but not
for eating. Five days in late December are set aside to pick, clean,
cull and carve giant varieties into animal and human figurines that
are placed in scenes for La Noche de Rábanos, or Night of the Radishes. The best tableaux—sprayed with water to stay fresh for mere
hours—win substantial prizes. Crowds numbering in the thousands
file by to have a look. All radishes for the competition are grown on
government land to meet the demand and are distributed fairly to

Radishes vary from bite-sized orbs to gargantuan roots in colours from black to red
to green to satisfy every cuisine. Photo: Simone McIsaac, Rootdown Organic Farm,
Pemberton, BC

give all competitors an equal chance. A recent harvest for carving? Twelve tons.

Green onions and radishes in a plethora of sizes, shapes and colours can be grown all over BC. Indeed, cooler temperatures combined with longer days in the northern part of the province make for perfect growing conditions for these vegetables. They show up in farmers' markets everywhere, a red-and-green sign of spring.

When buying BC radishes of the early spring variety, the sooner they get from the field to your kitchen (and your mouth), the better. Smaller is usually better—younger, milder, juicier. Green leafy tops should look fresh, not wilted, making them all the better to add to salads or cook like spinach. Before refrigerating your purchase, trim the leaves off the roots and rinse both tops and radishes clean, then drain before storing separately in bags in the crisper. They should last a week, but why wait? Set radishes out at lunch or before dinner with butter and coarse salt, to dip them the way the French do. Top buttered fresh bread with slices for an open-faced delight, Dutch-style, for breakfast. Or chase your beer with sliced radishes sprinkled with salt and chives, as the Germans do.

Cooking spring radishes has now become popular—braising, roasting or stewing them as you would larger winter daikon, mellowing their peppery taste. But for a spring dish with crunch and spice, I like to make a radish raita or tzatziki. It can be made with daikon but is ever so much prettier with bright red spring radishes. Chop up one bunch and sprinkle with salt. Let stand for twenty to thirty minutes. Drain and squeeze dry. Add about two tablespoons thinly sliced green onion tops, avoiding the white parts. Stir together one cup yogurt and one tablespoon lemon or lime juice and add to vegetables. Use as a side dish for hot curries, as a spread for crackers, bread or naan, or with grilled meats. Fresh and delightful, cooling with a bit of bite—perfect for spring.

Opposite: When ordinary people could finally afford to buy sugar to sweeten bitter rhubarb in the 1700s, the stalks began to take on a starring role in desserts. Photo: robertsre/Shutterstock.com

RELIABLE RHUBARB:
MADE FOR CANADA

As a child, I came to know rhubarb early. My family lived on the shores of Lake Superior back then, a land of relentless wind and blowing snow in winter. My sister and I spent hours out in it. We pulled on sweaters, snow pants, boots and jackets with hoods trimmed in fur. Mom wrapped long woollen scarves around our foreheads, then down and over our chins and noses, ending with a lopsided knot tied at the back of our heads. You'd think we were

heading out into the Arctic. We were as round as Russian nesting dolls but without the red cheeks—those came later.

We tramped all around the yard, leaving our footprints in the virgin white while searching for the highest drifts piled against the side of the house. Then we dug, flailing snow out behind us with frozen mittens, carving hideouts that were cozy and warm with our breath. And all the while we knew that below us, tucked into the ground next to the house, the rhubarb slept.

Rhubarb hibernates. It doesn't just rest, like other perennials; it sleeps like a bear in a den. It can withstand temperatures of minus thirty or worse, making it a valued friend of the North. In early spring, it pokes its green and red shoots out of the ground and grows like mad, shooting up sturdy stalks topped with giant leaves in even the shortest seasons. Each plant keeps this up for around fifteen years.

In places like Alaska, it was an early favourite of the first settlers. Russians brought rhubarb with them when they settled on Kodiak Island in 1784. Imagine eating something fresh in spring after a long hard winter of canned beans, shrivelled potatoes and goodness knows what else. During the 1920s, Henry Clark became known as the Rhubarb King for growing rhubarb that reached over 150 centimetres tall in the long daylight hours in Skagway, Alaska.

During our travels up in the Canadian North, my husband and I visited the astonishingly beautiful village of Atlin, tucked just inside BC close to the Yukon border. Once a popular tourist destination for ladies and gents in fancy dress who enjoyed paddlewheel boat rides on enormous Atlin Lake, it is a quiet place now but its beauty remains. We noticed that there were rhubarb plants everywhere: dotting yards, sprouting in gravel along the streets and pressing up against walls and in corners. Locals call it wild rhubarb because

Opposite: Hardy rhubarb is a friend of the North, stubbornly appearing year after year even in the harshest climates. It can be found growing all over BC. Photo: Sophie McAulay/Shutterstock.com

that's what it has become, and every spring they harvest the stalks to make chutneys, jams, cakes, muffins and pies. Visitors are welcome to take their pick but are warned to choose carefully and wash well, because the local dogs like it too.

Rhubarb was used as a medicine before it was a food. It likely showed up growing wild somewhere near the Bosporus or Volga River to start, but around 2700 BC the Chinese dried and ground the roots for use as a stomach remedy and laxative. They attempted to monopolize the source and trade, using the Russians—who had a Department of Rhubarb in the 1600s—as brokers. Later on, during the Opium Wars in the 1800s, the Chinese attempted to halt British opium imports into China by threatening to cut all tea and rhubarb exports to Britain, leaving them constipated and missing tea time. At least, that was the idea. It didn't turn out well for the Chinese as the British responded with cannon fire, and the rest, as they say, is history.

It was the price of sugar that changed everything for rhubarb. When people could afford to sweeten bitter rhubarb stalks in the late 1700s, it became popular in desserts. British Victorians embraced growing and eating it with gusto. Settlers carried it to North America, where it appeared in farmers' markets in the early 1800s. In her book *The First Four Years*, Laura Ingalls Wilder describes gathering stalks of the pie plant, a.k.a. rhubarb, to make dessert, which to her embarrassment was not the success she'd hoped for. Sour faces all around the table told her she'd forgotten to add one vital ingredient—sugar.

Rhubarb is grown all over the province and can be found in farmers' markets and grocery stores starting in April in the southern parts of BC, and a bit later up north. The season extends up until July. Search for stalks that are firm and have cut ends that look fresh. Remove all vestiges of leaves (which are poisonous) and cut into small chunks. If the stalks are really thick, cut them down the middle first, as with celery. If you are lucky enough to have too much rhubarb on hand, it is easy to freeze: just lay out cut rhubarb on baking sheets, freeze and bag or put in containers. It will keep for a year, or right up until the new crop appears next year.

As with most people, my favourite recipes use this vegetable as a fruit in desserts. But there are ways to enjoy rhubarb in savoury dishes too. My ridiculously large selection of cookbooks varies from year to year, but tucked away in a corner is a small gem—a gift from a friend who travelled around the world in the 1970s, no small feat at the time. She bought it in Afghanistan when peace and modernization gained an all-too-brief foothold. Inside this little book, which I treasure, lies a recipe for rhubarb *koresh*, or stew. Savoury recipes for rhubarb now dot the internet.

But my favourite rhubarb recipe is for pie, and it couldn't be simpler. Featured in the cookbook *Fresh Tarts* by Susan Mendelson (of Lazy Gourmet fame) and Deborah Roitberg, it's called "Grandma's Get-Yourself-a-Husband Pie." Family lore says it worked not only for Deborah's grandmother, but for her mother as well.

To find your own sweetheart, start with an unbaked pie shell in a 23-centimetre (9-inch) pie pan. For the filling, combine 3 eggs, 3 tablespoons flour and ⅞ cup sugar, and whisk until blended. Add 4 cups diced rhubarb and pour into pie shell. (Mixture will be gooey.) Bake at 425 degrees Fahrenheit for 10 minutes, then reduce to 325 degrees and bake 30 minutes longer. Serve with love.

You can also serve up your very own rhubarb. Any BC resident who has a neglected corner in a yard somewhere can grow this hardy plant, and it takes just one plant to provide enough for a couple of months' worth of delicious desserts every year. Buy a potted rhubarb from the nursery in the spring and plant as directed. Give it a drink every once in a while and leave it alone the first year. The second spring, stalks can be twisted off sparingly as desired, leaving enough behind to let the plant recover and start to nod off by midsummer. The third year and every year after that will present a bonanza. You can be a rhubarb king or queen too.

GRABBLING FOR NUGGETS

My mother-in-law's Sunday-night dinners in Ladner were legendary. Every week, lost souls, friends and relatives gathered at the house in the afternoon, knowing if they lingered long enough they would be sharing a meal. Even as a newcomer with recently acquired girlfriend status, I was embraced with warm hospitality. I was a little in awe of Eileen, who looked as if she belonged on a fashion runway more than in the kitchen, always perfectly coiffed, stylishly pant-suited and turned out in high heels. BC born and raised, she was an accomplished cook and a consummate hostess with a widely varied repertoire. She opened up new food worlds to me—a recent implant from colder eastern climes and a fresh-veggie tenderfoot.

One Sunday afternoon in June, Eileen decided to take me out, literally, on a field trip. She drove to a nearby friendly farmer's field, parked the Caddy at the edge of the road and led me down through the weedy ditch and up to the border of the field. How she managed this more gracefully than I while wearing high heels remains a mystery. Leafy green potato plants, perched on arrow-straight, raised earthen rows, stretched out as far as the eye could see. This was the first time I had stepped into a farmer's field, and it seemed extraordinarily orderly to me. We crouched down and stuck our fingers, then our hands, deep into the dry dirt at the bottom of the nearest row, wriggling our fingers and feeling around until we hit pay dirt: baby potatoes. We were, as it is officially called, grabbling, an apt term if there ever was one. I was enchanted.

Opposite: If spring weather is typically cool and damp, pink-eyed baby Warbas are ready to harvest starting in early June for five or more weeks of potato heaven. Photo: Michelle Peters-Jones for BCfresh

The nuggets we picked and ate that afternoon were grown from Warba seed potatoes. We snatched them as infants from the mother plants, leaving the matriarchs undisturbed. These savoury little spuds are picked and sold as babies, giving them their distinctive taste and texture: smooth, buttery and sweet. They are instantly recognizable by their white flesh, sunken pinkish eyes and thin, papery skins that easily peel away with a cloth or fingertips.

Now deemed an heirloom variety, Warbas were bred in an agricultural lab in Minnesota during the late 1920s. The aim was to pioneer a variety to yield an extra-early, plentiful harvest of new potatoes. No GMO fiddling (unknown at the time) was involved—just crossbreeding as farmers have done for thousands of years. Warbas fit the bill and turned out to be winners in the climate and soils of the Fraser Valley. By the 1940s the potatoes had become so popular with farmers and consumers in our province that they were called BC nuggets—as if they were ours alone. The rest of Canada was and is mostly BC-nuggetless. Those poor souls don't even know what they are missing—a blessing, really.

Beyond our realm, the only potatoes that compare in taste to these mini spuds are Jersey Royals, according to those who have tasted both. By law, only potatoes grown on the island of Jersey off the shores of France can be called by that name. Jersey farmers export around thirty thousand tons of them to the UK each year, promoting their own special potatoes grown in their own unique soil and climate—just like ours.

Warbas are grown in the Lower Mainland, in the Fraser Valley and on Vancouver Island, with smatterings cultivated all over the province. As with all spuds, the crop is started by planting pieces of last year's potatoes in the ground, each with an "eye" or two to sprout into a new plant—just as old potatoes try to do in your fridge or pantry. As the leafy foliage rises out of the ground, loose dirt is piled around and onto the plants, covering the lower leaves. This process, called hilling, is done to increase yield and prevent undesirable potato greening caused by sun exposure.

If the weather is typically cool and wet, baby Warbas are ready to harvest starting in early June for five or more weeks of potato heaven. If we are lucky, and the sun has bullied the clouds away to warm the soil more than usual in the spring, harvesting can begin as early as mid-May. Officially, Warbas are now called "new nuggets"—as in the first ones out of the ground—to differentiate them from the rest of the rabble. They grace produce sections and markets weeks ahead of any other Canadian-grown potatoes, including the new junior-sized varieties available in assorted colours later in the season.

I might miss out on catching the latest flick or acquiring the newest technological marvel, but I never miss the first baby Warbas to appear next to tired potatoes from last year. Handwritten signs may still identify them as BC nuggets—my preferred moniker. Worthy of eating again and again, the early to middle harvest—before the potatoes grow into larger-sized teenagers—is the best, I find. During the season, I admit to having meals consisting only of these tender little tatties (that's Scottish for potatoes) piled high on my

Paper-skinned or skinless new Warba potatoes simply require rinsing to prepare them for cooking—no peeling, ever. Photo: Lisa Bolton, Food Stylist

plate. I mostly skip rice, pasta and other carbs during the season to get my fill before they disappear.

Since they lack real skins, Warbas are short-lived once they leave their mothers. They store for only a few days in the fridge, so frequent trips to the grocery store or market are in order. The freshest specimens are hard and creamy white, without blemishes. It pays to be picky when buying to get the best taste.

To enjoy the bounty, Warbas need no special attention: rub any dirt off (no need to remove all the papery skin), cut in halves or quarters (unless they are really tiny) and stick in a pot with some water to steam until tender. These little taters may take longer to cook than later-season potatoes, so patience and pot watching are required. When fork tender, drain and pour onto a plate, add butter, salt and pepper and dig in. To add a grilled flavour, wrap cooked potatoes in foil with butter and throw on the barbecue while the meat is cooking.

Baby Warba potatoes are stolen from below unsuspecting leafy mother plants by grabbling—digging into the dirt—leaving the matriarchs undisturbed. Photo: Brian Faulkner, BCfresh

It is difficult to do anything but eat these gems hot and straight from the pot or barbecue. But to gild the lily, they make a divine potato salad as well. There are as many recipes for potato salad as there are grandmothers on this earth, and any one of them will taste better made with BC nuggets. Here is a simple one that brings out the taste of the main ingredient: Cook a potful of potatoes as above. Drain and spread out to cool on a cutting board or counter. Slap any hand that comes close "just to have a taste." When cool, cut into smaller chunks. Mix 1 tablespoon each of regular mustard and white vinegar with $1/3$ cup of mayonnaise until smooth, then pour over and stir into 5 to 6 cups of potatoes. Add chopped green onion—a seasonal green   and salt and pepper to taste. Attempt to make enough to refrigerate leftovers for lunch the next day, keeping in mind that the attractions of a late-night snack may override all good intentions.

Repeat, often, during the season.

Almost any potato recipe tastes better made with sweet and creamy Warbas, an heirloom variety bred in the 1920s that became wildly successful in BC. Photo: Lisa Bolton, Food Stylist

GIVE PEAS A CHANCE

The hot sun beats down on my shoulders, wrapping me in its warm embrace as I stand in my garden inspecting the snow and snap peas. Planted early in the spring, the vines now form a wall 150 centimetres high, supported by countless fine tendrils reaching out and clinging to the sagging mesh trellis behind. A few errant stems have fallen forward, and I carefully raise them up, ever so gently wrapping any tendrils I can find around the mesh with my fingers. I know that within an hour, these delicate anchors will be firmly wound, curling like a toddler's arm around a mother's knee. Magic.

Every day I head to the pea patch to search for pods hidden among the pale green leaves and white blossoms, ready for eating. When I find them, they go straight from the plant into my mouth, crisp and juicy, and I rejoice in the taste of one of the first green vegetables of the season that is not a leaf.

It was not that long ago that for many of us North Americans, peas meant round green things rolling around on a plate, unsung and underappreciated. Restaurants avoided them because it was hard for diners to eat them without using fingers or knives to get them where they needed to go—difficult to accomplish with aplomb. These round versions are shelling peas and must be removed from tough inedible pods before eating—a time-consuming task best accomplished by machine or while sitting on the front porch with a basketful of pods and endless time to spare.

Shelling peas are one of the oldest cultivated crops we humans have. No one can really decide where they first grew—Burma, India,

Opposite: In 1976, snow peas were crossed with ordinary shelling peas to produce a stellar combination: the snap pea, a sweet mange-tout with unsurpassed flavour. Photo: Nadezhda Nesterova/Shutterstock.com

Egypt or the Middle East—or even when. They date back to around ten thousand years ago. For most of their history, peas were left to mature and dry in the field in their pods before they were shelled. These hard yellow versions not only make more sense in the *Princess and the Pea* fairy tale, but were a staple for the hungry that could be stored dry for months, like grains or beans. The rhyme "Pease porridge hot, pease porridge cold, pease porridge in the pot, nine days old" describes the practice of cooking dried peas in broth or water over the fire for hours—hot at night, cold by morning and topping up the pot for nine days. Hardly appetizing.

Though people did eat shelling peas green, fresh and immature here and there, it was King Louis XIV of France who changed the course of pea history in the late 1600s. Louis settled for only the best when it came to dinner. His Versailles abode included a large *potager du roi* (literally, "vegetable garden of the king"), tended by thirty gardeners to provide the king's chefs with the freshest produce of the season. A new hybrid grown in this garden, a tender and sweet variety called *petit pois*, was favoured by Louis and became all the rage in Europe. Table talk revolved around peas, and snacking on them, even at bedtime, became a fad, a "madness," for the ladies of the court.

Nowadays, shelled green peas are stars of the frozen section in the grocery store, tasting closer to fresh than any other frozen vegetable. Only 5 to 10 percent of the harvest is sold fresh, in pods, mostly at farmers' markets and stands. For best taste, especially when nibbled raw straight out of the pod—the way Louis liked them—these peas need to get from the field into your hands *tout de suite*.

How fortunate we are that our pea choices have expanded. Snow peas—flat translucent beauties with tiny peas inside—have a more recent, though still mysterious, history. Popular in Asian cooking, they may have started out in Europe in the sixteenth century before making their way to China, where they came into their own in the garden and in the wok. Snap peas—full-size sweet peas filling out tender edible pods—are newcomers. In 1976, a shelling pea was crossbred with a snow pea to produce a stellar combination, showcasing the best qualities of both parents with a bonus: high sugar content. Both snow and snap peas, sometimes called mange-tout—meaning "eat it all," both pea and pod—are delightful additions to our meals. How did we ever get along without them?

Peas are easy to grow, even for the home gardener. All three types—snow, snap and shelling—grow well all over the province. Planted "as soon as the soil can be worked" in spring—that means

Opposite: Crunchy snow peas are available fresh in early summer from farmers' markets and at roadside stands, often picked the same day from a field nearby. Photo: iStock.com/lightofchairat

neither soggy nor frozen—peas produce their bounty about two months later. Farmers sow successively, planting new seeds every ten to fourteen days to lengthen the harvest. As cool-weather aficionados, peas begin to fade in the intense sun and heat of midsummer. For most of BC, that means fresh local peas show up in June and July, or even earlier in the warmest corners of our province.

When you buy peas at farmers' markets or stands, chances are they've been picked from a field not far away that same morning. It's almost like having your own garden. Peas should be crisp, solid green and unblemished. Bag and store in the fridge to stop the conversion of sugar into starch, and use within a few days. Snow and snap peas may need to have their strings removed unless they are the newest varieties. I snap off the ends and pull down to remove the strings from both sides of the pods just before using.

Out in my garden, I try not to eat all the sweet plump snap peas right there and then. If I manage to bring any inside, my favourite way to eat them is raw, with a dip. It doesn't get any better, for the dip—any dip—or the peas. Those that pass this gauntlet, along with any tender snow peas I have gathered, go into salads. Just before dinner, I toss a small handful or two into boiling water, wait till it comes to a boil again—mere seconds—then chill immediately under cold running water and drain. This makes them ultra-tender and the brightest of greens. I add the pods, whole or halved, to a simple green salad dressed with a mild vinaigrette to bring out their divine sweetness. Even Louis XIV would be pleased.

ON BECOMING A LOCAVORE

In British Columbia, our foodshed—where we get our food—is global. We buy fruits and vegetables grown in China (garlic), Peru (asparagus), Italy (kiwi), South Africa (apples), Korea (mushrooms), Morocco (clementines), New Zealand (apples), Chile (blueberries) and California and Mexico (almost everything), just to name a few. Unlike our watershed, our foodshed is not local by any definition.

So what exactly defines a food as local? It depends. When it comes to fruits and vegetables, I can pick beans and tomatoes out of my garden in Whistler—the zero-mile diet. But local offerings also include a wonderful selection of veggies grown in the hot dry climate and fertile soil of the Pemberton Valley, thirty kilometres down the road. And I embrace the wonderful assortment of berries from the Lower Mainland that appear at our farmers' market all summer, two thousand kilometres closer than any from southern California.

In their book *The 100-Mile Diet: A Year of Local Eating*, BC authors J.B. MacKinnon and Alisa Smith attempted to eat food sourced from within one hundred miles of their Vancouver home for one year. It was tough. Would I restrict myself to a certain distance? Not necessarily. In our province, we are fortunate to have a variety of different climates and landscapes that lend themselves to growing a remarkable variety of fruits and vegetables, and I want to take advantage of that diversity. From my point of view, local produce includes peaches from the Okanagan that arrive at our farmers' market and grocery stores in July, even though that's four hundred kilometres away. Compared with California—the source of well-travelled, flavourless peaches—the Okanagan offers fruit that tastes better and, to me, is local. I consider myself a fruit and vegetable locavore because I make every effort to eat produce grown as close as possible to where I live.

By experimenting with diverse and unusual varieties, small local farmers help to maintain the biodiversity of seed banks, which are vital to our future. Photo: Michael Levy, Flat Earth Photography

In the end, we all make our own choices. If you live in Prince George, buying locally grown produce is going to be different—and trickier—than if you live in Victoria. One thing is sure: for everyone, becoming a locavore can be a challenge. It's just so much simpler to buy everything in the grocery store. Is it really worth all the fuss to eat locally grown produce? What are the reasons to make the effort to reduce the size of your vegetable and fruit foodshed? It turns out there are quite a few.

FLAVOUR

It was taste that initially set me on the road to becoming a locavore. Growing up in a time and place where fresh produce was as rare as a vine-ripened tomato in January, encountering the flavour of local fruits and vegetables after moving to BC was nothing short of a revelation. To me, taste alone is reason enough to seek out local foods that are in season, fresh, delicious and nutritious because they have not spent the best days of their picked lives in a semi truck or airplane. And travelling fruits and vegetables are often picked before their prime, the better to withstand long journeys—but the worse for flavour. The local bounty at roadside stands or farmers' markets is usually picked less than twenty-four hours before—putting us only one step away from the farmer's field and ensuring we get the harvest at its peak.

CONNECTION

When I buy from the farmers' market or roadside stand, it helps me to understand what grows close to where I live, and when. I talk directly to farmers about what is in season, right now. We muse over how the weather is affecting their harvests. I notice the dirt under their fingernails as they weigh my purchase and take my money. I feel a connection to the land and the farmer who toils to feed me. Today, it's easy to feel disconnected from where our food comes from and how it is grown because it's just there, perfect and uniform, in the supermarket all year round. In her book *Animal, Vegetable, Miracle: A Year of Food Life*, Barbara Kingsolver says we now

Buying locally grown food helps us feel connected to the land and the farmers who toil to feed us, creating a community in which we support each other. Photo: Highwaystarz Photography/Istock.com

mistakenly think the most important part of where we get our food is the grocery store—and we forget about all that goes before. Big business has come between us and those who grow our food. Buying locally grown fruits and vegetables can reconnect us with the land, the plants and the farmer in a meaningful, satisfying way, helping to create a community in which we support each other.

ECONOMICS

Buying locally grown produce keeps dollars in our neighbourhoods instead of allowing them to disappear into corporate pockets far away. When purchasing directly from the growers at markets, at roadside stands or through weekly harvest baskets, the farmer gets the entire economic benefit. Ninety-eight percent of farms in BC are family owned—and buying their homegrown bounty encourages them to continue to work hard to feed us all. They deserve our gratitude and support.

FOOD SECURITY

Financial success for farmers also helps keep agricultural land from turning into something else. In BC, only 5 percent of our mountainous province is good for growing crops, and we cannot afford to lose any of it. What if the present food system broke down in some way? Keeping our agricultural land intact and sustaining the farmers who know how to grow what we need is important for our food security in the future, especially when considering what climate change may bring. Most of us in BC feel a deep and heartfelt connection to our rivers, oceans and mountains—we need to feel the same way about the farmland that feeds us.

SUSTAINABILITY

BC farms selling fruits and vegetables directly to consumers often make efforts to be as sustainable as possible. They grow a variety of crops—avoiding the monoculture of vast agribusinesses—and steer clear of GMO seeds. They are often interested in ecological, organic farming, and caring for the land they depend upon is a priority. Though not all are certified organic, a process that can be expensive and time-consuming, a recent study done by the University of Guelph found that 100 percent of Canadian farms in a survey that were growing vegetables for weekly harvest box programs practised at least some organic farming techniques. This doesn't mean that all small farms are sustainable and all large farms are not, but buying locally means we can choose which ones we want to grow our food and help encourage good stewardship of our farmland for future generations.

CARBON FOOTPRINT

This one's tricky. Most of the carbon that is emitted from growing food comes from farming methods, not transportation. Fertilizer use releases nitrous oxide, which is almost three hundred times more potent as a greenhouse gas than carbon dioxide. Methane released from ruminants like cows is twenty-five times more potent than CO_2. So while vast amounts of strawberries packed into an airplane may be a fairly efficient use of fossil fuel, the carbon footprint depends greatly on how those berries were raised in distant lands. And while the toll paid in emissions with long-distance travel may be less than originally thought, the carbon price is not zero. It depends on the method of travel as well. Transportation by rail or sea is less carbon intensive than air and truck transport, but how many vegetables and fruits travel by train or ship? We may chose to reduce our carbon footprint substantially by eating less red meat, but we can reduce it further by eating locally, sustainably grown food.

BIODIVERSITY

Small farmers are more likely to try growing heirloom and unique varieties. They are passionate in their quest to offer us delightful choices in size, shape, colour and taste—something new and interesting that we'll never see in the grocery store. Local farmers care about flavour, not stamina, and are able to offer us tender varieties that do not travel well. Industrial, monoculture farming aims for volume, low price and toughness, the better to bounce around in the back of a truck for a thousand kilometres. We are quickly losing our seed heritage as older, unique fruits and vegetables become lost to us, sometimes forever. Buying locally from smaller farmers is the best way to maintain the vitality and diversity of our seed banks.

FOOD SAFETY

When we buy directly from the farmer, or find locally grown food at the grocery store, we know where our food comes from. What do we know of farming in Peru or Mexico? Since local produce has not passed through as many handlers as fruits and vegetables that cross multiple borders, there is less chance for safety issues to arise. Farm to table with fewer or no middlemen—what could be better?

Is it worth making the effort to become a locavore? We all have to decide for ourselves, but for me, it just feels like the right thing to do.

SUMMER

STRAWBERRY FIELDS
ARE NOT FOREVER

There is one day in June that holds a special place in the hearts of those who live or work in the village of Pemberton, just north of Whistler. It is the day of the Strawberry Tea. The exact date varies year to year depending on when local strawberries reach perfection, which in turn depends upon the weather. Mother Nature holds all the cards. But when the time is right—usually mid-June—Pembertonians are treated to strawberries, picked that morning in nearby fields, topped with whipped cream. The ladies of the Women's Institute, a venerable organization founded in 1940, serve up the treat every year at the Pemberton Museum, but even better, they deliver.

At workplaces around town, pens are laid to rest, fingers pause over keyboards, meetings wrap up and coffee breaks happen when a delivery—preordered with the ladies—arrives at the door. After all, when a dish of sweet ripe strawberries and cream appears, it needs attention—pronto.

Not only is this a fundraiser for the Pemberton Museum and other local organizations, it is a celebration of summer, strawberries and the fields and farmers of the beautiful Pemberton Valley.

It was Thomas Wolsey, cardinal and chancellor to King Henry VIII, who supposedly first came up with the idea of combining strawberries with cream in one tasty dish in 1509. In reality, it was probably one of the poor souls working in the kitchen to feed the six hundred people usually staying at Hampton Court, Wolsey's personal palace, who dreamt up the delightful pairing.

Opposite: The best-tasting strawberries are local—red, ripe, sweet and just picked, perfect for immediate gratification. Photo: Alison Stevens/Unsplash

This delicious treat stood the test of time and almost four hundred years later was featured at the first Wimbledon tennis tournament in 1877, conveniently held right in the middle of strawberry season. Now an established tradition, over thirty thousand kilograms of fresh local berries are served up each year to tennis fans.

As with every plant we eat, strawberries started out in the wild, and they're still there. Like in my woodland yard. For hundreds of years, varieties of wild strawberries grew all over Europe, North America and parts of South America. Not being fussy, plants popped up in gravel, in sand and in the woods. On this side of the ocean, Indigenous people picked them to eat fresh and to dry. Europeans transplanted them from the woodlands into their gardens so successfully that in the fourteenth century, Charles V of France had 1,200 strawberry plants in his royal plot. He probably had six hundred people to feed too.

The trouble was, wild strawberries, though tasty, were small. Things changed in the eighteenth century when a Chilean variety—brought home by a wandering French spy—was crossed with a North American variety that had found its way into French gardens. The modern strawberry, larger and more productive, was born. Human fiddling (not GMO tampering), still ongoing, remains an interesting experiment, as strawberries are complicated: they can be girls or boys, or both, and reproduce by seeds (about two hundred per berry) or runners—stems that grow out from the mother plant to start a baby plant nearby. And botanically, they are not really berries at all. In a word, strawberries are special.

When BC strawberries appear it means summer is upon us. Usually they show up mid-June, but in the warmest parts of the province, they have appeared as early as the first two weeks of May if our spring has been unseasonably hot and sunny. Harvesting, a back-breaking job, is done by hand and lasts a glorious four to six weeks, again depending on the weather. The pleasure can be prolonged with ever-bearing varieties, which produce smaller harvests twice a year. But nothing matches the bonanza of June strawberries.

The best strawberries are local—and freshly picked, which means U-pick, or buying straight off the field or in a market that same day. There's no way around it. Berries should be picked with the leafy green cap and a bit of stem attached. They are at their sweetest when they are deep red and softer than longer-lasting underripe specimens. Unlike tree fruits, berries do not ripen after picking. And each year is different in berry sweetness, yield and size.

An early fan, King Charles V of France grew 1,200 strawberry plants in his garden in the 1300s to ensure an ample supply for royal feasts. Photo: Tim UR/Shutterstock.com

Every year, I head up to Pemberton to pick strawberries in June. But first, I consider the weather. Berries flourish in the sun, day after day. Steady rain is undesirable, stunting growth and encouraging mould. So I pick my day. I phone the farm too, to see if the picking is good. I gather family members to join me. I want enough berries for jam, for freezing and, best of all, for fresh eating.

One year I took my daughter, an extreme berry lover, and her best buddy, both eleven years old, along for the picking. We headed into the fields good and early. Picking low-lying strawberries is hard work, and we started by bending over at the waist, then kneeling, then crouching, and finally plunking ourselves down in the dusty silt to find perfect berries hidden under the leaves—a treasure hunt for rubies. Periodic quality testing was in order. The picking was good, the berries large and plentiful, so we filled several ice cream buckets before the heat of the sun beat us out of the field.

Over thirty thousand kilograms of local strawberries, topped with cream, are served up every year to fans at the Wimbledon tennis tournament—a tradition since 1877. Photo: Nannycz/Shutterstock.com

On the way home, the girls sat in the back, pails heaped with red jewels sitting between them. I had one beside me too, of course. As we headed down the highway, windows wide open, blasts of air whipped our hair around our faces wildly. Heat settled on us like a blanket. Then we started to eat, biting into one impossibly sweet and juicy morsel after another, throwing the green tops out the window for the wind to snatch out of our fingers. My daughter didn't think twice about partaking—what else would anyone do with berries beckoning beside you? Her friend needed convincing—just a little— as berries were usually washed before eating in her world. But these berries had not been sprayed, and besides, a little Pemberton dirt never hurt anyone. We decided they were the best strawberries we'd ever tasted, still warm from the sun, and we insisted each one was better than the last. We were giddy with strawberries and summer.

Strawberries can be grown all over BC, though most of the commercial growers are concentrated in the Okanagan, on Vancouver Island and in the Fraser Valley. When warm summer temperatures and sunshine appear, look for local strawberries, buy with wild abandon and enjoy them while they last.

Refrigerate berries as soon as possible and wash only just before eating. Local ripe strawberries do not stand the test of time as well as those California cousins bred for long-distance travel, so seize the day and enjoy them morning, noon and night. If there are enough berries, make freezer jam, which tastes incredibly fresh in March. Still more berries? Hull (cut off the green bits), wash, dry on paper towels on the counter (take a photo to keep this marvellous image in mind), pop onto cookie sheets to freeze, then bag.

If possible, try to keep enough berries for strawberry shortcake after dinner—the final pièce de résistance. Supermarkets sell plain shortcake but it's easy to do better. To make a cake in a flash, drop 1 egg in a 1-cup measuring cup, fill ¾ full with milk, then add corn oil up to 1 cup (about ¼ cup). Pour into a bowl and beat with a whisk until mixed. Add ½ cup sugar, 1 cup flour and 1 heaping teaspoon of baking powder. Whisk again and pour into a greased 20-by-20-centimetre (8-by-8-inch) pan. Bake at 350 degrees Fahrenheit for 20–25 minutes or until firm. Let cool. Cut into 9 squares, and slice each horizontally to make a top and bottom. Beat 1 cup whipping cream until peaks form, adding 1–2 teaspoons icing sugar to taste if you prefer a sweeter version. Alternatively, buy one of those handy squirt cans at the store. Lay berries plus dollops of whipped cream between the cake layers and again on top—the more, the better. A divine dessert that would surely pass muster with the cardinals and kings of Hampton Court, the tennis champs at Wimbledon and the people of Pemberton.

CHERRY CHAMPIONS

The appearance of cherries marks the beginning of the tree fruit season, a joyous romp through one fruit after another—cherries, then apricots, peaches, plums and finally pears and apples. An occasion worthy of celebration indeed.

No matter what part of the province we may be passing through in June and July, my husband and I keep a sharp lookout and scan the roadsides for handwritten signs proclaiming "Cherries for Sale." Sometimes it's just a solitary table set up on vacant asphalt, with a young entrepreneur—an orchardist's daughter perhaps—babysitting the impossibly beautiful crimson crop, freshly picked that

British Columbia is a cherry champion—famous outside its borders for a consistently sweet and juicy crop grown in the hot dry valleys of the Interior. Photo: Inma Ibáñez/Unsplash

morning. We veer off at every opportunity to have a gander, casing out the cherries like kicking tires on a car. We point, we deliberate, then we pounce.

We transfer whatever we buy into a plastic bag, search for a water tap to rinse the find and then head back to the car. The bag sits between our seats, open and available. We toss them into our mouths and bite down on one perfect, sweet, juicy cherry after another, throwing stems and pits aside. It seems the sun is always shining during these feasts, the heat pressing through the windows as we cruise down the highway. Sun, heat and cherries—a match made in heaven.

BC cherries have a sterling international reputation for being consistently large and sweet. Increasing quantities now make their way to demanding customers in China. But growers want to keep British Columbians happy too. The BC Cherry Association says that if consumers (that's us) insist on local rather than Washington State cherries in grocery stores, they can make greater inroads with the big boys—supermarket chains—to stock more BC beauties for us to buy.

Cherries have been a success story in our province since the late 1800s, flourishing in the favourable climate and soil of the Okanagan, Similkameen and Kootenay Valleys. Back then, British immigrants were encouraged to buy land and live the life of gentleman orchardists with plenty of time for leisurely pursuits. Tennis on the grass. Tea and crumpets at four. Glowing reports made their way back to the old country describing trees so laden with fruit that the branches had to be supported. Reality proved to be slightly more taxing. Clearing land and waiting several years for trees to produce decent harvests required more patience and hard labour than originally advertised.

Nevertheless, it wasn't long before cherry boom time hit the Kootenay Valley, where plentiful harvests, famous for their flavour, made their way to the Prairies, Washington State and the rest of the province. Disaster struck in 1933 when little cherry disease appeared—

still a serious concern today. The source and spread of this affliction, which causes cherries to be small, flavourless and oddly shaped, was a mystery for years. The possible villain? A couple of imported ornamental—and diseased—Japanese cherry trees smuggled illegally into a private garden near Nelson. Apple mealy bugs took it from tree to tree, and over thirty thousand trees had to be uprooted and destroyed. Cherries are still grown in the Creston Valley, but in other areas, like around Kaslo, the orchards have pretty well vanished.

Because little cherry disease is now understood, it can be studied and controlled to protect harvests in BC, and planting ornamental cherries—trees with almost non-existent fruits and showy blossoms—is still restricted in the Okanagan, Similkameen and Kootenay Valleys. A lesson learned while paradise was almost lost.

There are two main types of cherries: sweet, for fresh eating; and sour, for processing into pie fillings, juice and jams. Since 95 percent of sweet cherries grown in Canada come from BC, showing up in markets, roadsides and stands soon after picking, we get the freshest and the best. We also corner the market in cherry breeds as 80 percent of the world's harvests are grown from varieties crossbred in the Summerland Research and Development Centre in the Okanagan. We are, it seems, the cherry champions of the world. Let's take a bow.

As with every plant we eat, the weather has an obvious say in quality, quantity and timing of the harvest, but it is especially true when it comes to cherries. An early, warm spring means we enjoy them sooner, while a late, cool spring means we have to wait longer than usual for these treats. Our provincial geography plays a role too. The first cherries of the year come from Osoyoos, in the far south of the Okanagan Valley. Harvests continue to arrive in sequence, continuing north through places like Oliver and Penticton, followed by Naramata and Kelowna. When you come across the very first cherries of the season, casually ask, "Do these come from Osoyoos?" If you get this right, you'll feel almost as if you'd picked the cherries yourself. To feel closer to where your food comes from, every time you buy BC cherries, ask where they were grown.

Orchardists in BC can pick and choose what varieties to grow, like Bing, Skeena, Lapin, Sweetheart, Chelan, Staccato, Satin and Lambert, to name a few. Because they blossom and produce fruit at slightly different times, one after another, we can enjoy local cherries right up until mid-August. Harvests are picked by hand but first have to dodge rain, which causes skins to split, and birds, who like cherries just as much as we do.

Unlike other stone fruits, such as peaches, cherries do not continue to ripen after picking. That means they are at their prime when plucked, fully ripened, from the tree and eaten on the spot—unfortunately not an option for most of us. When buying, look for fully ripe cherries that are an intense, dark crimson, except for Rainiers, which are lighter and yellow/red. They should be firm—no soft spots—and still have their stems attached. Avoid those with cracks, showing rain damage. Cherries need to be refrigerated, unwashed, as soon as possible and should be eaten sooner rather than later. When it comes to cherries, immediate gratification is always the wisest course.

Most people have little desire to actually do anything with cherries except eat them fresh, one luscious morsel at a time. Recipes are not as plentiful as for other fruits. Why fight this sensible preference? For dessert, serve fresh cherries, stems on, pits in, arranged on a glass plate (crystal would be nice) beside the most sinful dark chocolates you can find. Expect the same appreciation as if you had spent hours baking. Bask in it anyway.

If you end up with too many cherries—a pleasant problem—rinse, drain, remove stems, lay on cookie sheets to freeze and then put into bags or containers. They will last until next year's crop comes in. To use, slightly thaw, squeeze to remove pits and add to smoothies all winter to kindle summer memories and help stave off withdrawal until next season.

THE BERRY PATCH

I earned my berry-picking stripes early when my family lived in Michipicoten Harbour, an isolated hamlet on the shores of Gitche Gumee—that's Lake Superior—in Northern Ontario. Back then, the Trans-Canada Highway was but a dream, and access to our neck of the woods was by train only. My mother often took my sister and me, both preschoolers at the time, out to pick tiny wild blueberries on low-lying bushes carpeting open areas between wind-stunted trees—a rugged Canadian landscape celebrated in paintings by the Group of Seven artists. Mom kept up a constant stream of loud conversation to keep the bears away, or so she says. I was happily oblivious. It must have been slow going as small children do not make good berry pickers, but we—that is, my mother—picked enough to freeze for pies during the long cold winters. Later, we repeated the experience in Northern Quebec, our foreheads greased with solid-stick 6-12 insect repellent to ward off blackflies as we collected tart blue treasures from bushes covering the sandy barrens. Being older, we were actually expected to add to the harvest if we wanted blueberry pies to keep coming out of the oven on those dark winter nights, flavour reminders of pale sun-washed late-summer days.

A veritable smorgasbord of wild, native berries grows in BC, up the entire coast and into the Interior, including blueberries, raspberries, blackberries, huckleberries and many others. First Nations have relied on them for thousands of years, eating the bounty fresh and drying the surplus for winter use. Careful selection and crossbreeding (no GMO tampering) of wild varieties found throughout

Opposite: Berries are big business in BC and provide a taste parade, starting with strawberries, then raspberries, blackberries and currants, and finally blueberries, to delight us all summer long. Photo: Tiago Faifa/Unsplash

the Northern Hemisphere have provided growers with the cultivated berry plants that feed us today. Every sweet morsel we buy at the farmers' market had its genetic beginnings in the woodlands or clearings out in the wild.

Berries have become big business in our province—partly because we just can't seem to get enough of them, and partly because some areas of the province are perfect for growing them. Not only does BC grow large quantities of berries, but processing and packing takes place here as well. That means locally grown harvests are sorted for freezing, or juice and jam production. When buying strawberries, raspberries, blueberries or cranberries in the freezer aisle at the grocery store, watch for "BC grown" or "Grown in Canada" labelling to make sure you are getting local fruit for eating all winter long. Many Lower Mainland berry farms do their own freezing, so buying directly from the grower is easy too.

British Columbia also has its own established breeding and research programs for berries; for instance, take black and red currants, which are catching on fast here. These berries have been more popular in Europe and Britain than in North America as they had a nasty reputation in the past for passing on disease to our pine trees. But disease-free varieties like Stikine, Whistler and Blackcomb have now been bred in BC. Perfect for our unique climate and soils, they are being cultivated for fresh eating or processing into jams, jellies and juices.

The Pacific Agri-Food Research Centre in Agassiz, which fine-tunes raspberry species, has a tradition of using First Nation names for new varieties. They have brought us the Chemainus, Malahat, Chilliwack, Skeena, Nootka and Qualicum raspberry cultivars, all discovered and homegrown right here in our province. Our very own berries made in BC—worthy of sustained applause.

Most commercially grown raspberries are raised in the Lower Mainland and Fraser Valley, where 175 farmers toil to satisfy us, growing 85 percent of Canada's total harvest. Ten percent of the crop is hand-picked for fresh eating directly into containers, which appear in roadside stands, markets and grocery stores, often within twenty-four hours, for us to buy. The remaining harvest is shaken and combed off the tall prickly bushes by machines to be packed for freezing or processing.

Blueberries overwhelm raspberries in harvest size and popularity in our province. About seven hundred farmers produce seventy-seven million kilograms of the berries annually, putting BC in third place for world production of highbush or cultivated berries. These high-yield bushes are relative newcomers on the agricultural scene. They were bred in the early 1900s from those back-breaking lowbush blueberries we picked back east. Different varieties ripen at different times to extend the season. British Columbia is a blueberry superstar, growing 95 percent of Canada's crop.

Though most of our cultivated blueberry crops are grown in the Fraser Valley—especially Richmond and Delta—farmers can be found in places like Ladysmith, Sumas, Lone Butte, Powell River, Kelowna, Duncan and Prince George too. That means we can find locally grown, hand-picked blueberries for fresh eating close to home almost all over the province.

Blackberries are also commercially grown in the Fraser Valley, where farmers wisely grow thornless types to hand-pick for fresh eating. The pesky Himalayan blackberry, brought to BC in 1885, has made itself at home along with the native variety and now grows all along the coast and in the Okanagan. A thorny, gangly bush, it suffocates other plants and is so dense it has actually been used as fencing to keep animals and people away. It has been declared an invasive species. The berries produce thousands of seeds within every square metre of bush, making control a daunting task. Picking from these bushes provides a cache of delicious berries with a price: scratches and scrapes from fighting with the prickly branches. But then again, they're free.

Depending on the weather, berry season in BC begins with strawberries in June, followed by raspberries, blackberries and currants in July, and blueberries, which start in July but can hang on into the fall. All types thrive in hot, sunny conditions, so if we have an early, warm spring, the parade of berries starts sooner. Persistent good weather can speed things up so that harvests edge up to one another and overlap—meaning we can have a selection of red, blue and black baubles arrayed at farmers' markets and roadside stands all at once.

Many farms offer U-pick as well—my personal favourite. Perhaps it was my early training that made me a lifelong U-picker. What a delight it is to gather handfuls of dusky blueberries at North Arm Farm in Pemberton while listening to the nearby aspens whisper and flutter in the wind. Or to pluck tayberries, a raspberry-blackberry cross, on tranquil Westham Island, a rural sanctuary surrounded by urbanity. Or to search out huckleberry jewels in my woodland backyard while watching out for bears as my mother did long ago. Even picking prickly raspberries in Richmond or thorny roadside blackberries on Bowen Island is satisfying, in spite of the inevitable war wounds. The berry patch is a warm, quiet and peaceful place where time slows almost to a standstill, a contrast from our hectic, everyday world. A meditative experience with a bonus: fresh fruit to feast on at home.

When heading into the raspberry or blackberry patch to pick, be sure to wear long sleeves and pants—no shorts allowed—to battle the prickly canes, spiders and bugs. Ripe blackberries are plump and dark. Raspberries, on the other hand, should not be too dark or pale, or too soft or hard. Think like Goldilocks. Perfect, ripe, sweet berries should easily come off the core. Fill containers halfway to avoid squashed berries, and keep them in the shade while picking. Blueberries are a snap to pick and quickly fill pails much to everyone's satisfaction. Avoid unripe reddish berries, and choose firm blues that have a natural silvery sheen.

All berries need to go straight into the fridge at home. No washing until just before partaking. Berries do not ripen after picking, so eating often and early is the best policy. Freezing is easy too—just rinse, dry on towels and spread over cookie sheets to freeze before bagging. Alternatively, freeze unwashed and rinse just before eating. I simply cannot do winter without my frozen BC sunshine—a personal stash of berries.

These days, fresh berries have worked their way into our meals in a myriad of ways as we take their stellar nutritional reputation to heart. One of my favourite pairings is rich lemon yogurt topped with fresh blueberries—a divine combo, perfect for company and as good as any cheesecake, with a fraction of the guilt and effort.

Frozen is as good as fresh when it comes to tossing a handful of berries into muffins and pancakes. Apple pie and apple crisp acquire a rich colour and flavour boost with a sprinkling of blueberries, with no need to alter the recipes. It's easy to make whole berry syrup too. Put one-half cup of fresh or frozen berries in a saucepan. Use one type or a mixture of berries. I even toss in a few huckleberries from the backyard if I have them. Stir one teaspoon of cornstarch into one-third cup of water until milky smooth, add to pot and cook over medium-high heat, stirring constantly, until mixture comes to a boil. Turn down to a simmer, and continue to stir while it's burbling. When the liquid turns translucent and jewel-like, it's done. Add sweetener (just a little) if desired: honey, maple syrup or sugar. Perfect for topping pancakes, cheesecake or ice cream, and gorgeous too.

How do we love BC berries? Let me count the ways…

Haricots Verts Extraordinaire

There was a time when I thought the best green beans came in a can; "frenched," they called them, sliced lengthwise into smithereens, with mysterious soft bits of red sprinkled throughout—was it pimento? I don't think I met a fresh green bean until I was twenty, and it involved a trip across the ocean. When I finally encountered the uncanned sort, I was ripe for a conversion.

Back then, it was terribly *de rigueur* for young adults to go to Europe and bum around with no particular place to go for at least a month. Most of us had never been anywhere much, and neither had our parents. We were the first. Just owning a passport seemed exotic and adventurous.

When my turn came to go in August 1972, I stood, clutching a ticket to London in my hand inside the gate at Vancouver International Airport, trying to act nonchalant while Mom and Dad stood smiling and waving on the other side of the glass wall—airport security being non-existent at the time. It was all an act; I was terrified and felt desperately alone. I had plans to meet my sister in Nice—a lifeline.

Two weeks later, slightly less fearful and done with jolly old England, I dodged too-friendly types in the Paris train station to catch the overnight train south. Morning found me standing in the aisle, swaying with the train and staring out the murky window at the glittering Mediterranean. The stocky, dark-haired matron standing next

Opposite: Tasty multicoloured string beans can be grown all over BC and appear in markets, roadside stands and groceries from late June until early September. Photo: Paul Pellegrino/Shutterstock.com

to me, dressed all in black, looked like she had never shaved her legs in her life. My heart swelled. I was a traveller.

My sister was well acquainted with everything French by the time I met up with her in Nice that day. At least, it seemed that way to me. She had spent a glorious month housed in the École Nationale Supérieure d'Arts de Nice high above the old town, in striking buildings of glass and metal, taking a studio art course. That evening, she took me down into the narrow, twisting streets (hosed out every morning, she said) lined with ancient, tiny shops with people living above. We entered a small restaurant with blocky wooden tables and chairs arranged on the tile floor, topped with checkered tablecloths. I felt like I was in a Van Gogh painting.

My sister ordered *salade niçoise* for both of us—a novelty to me but not to her. There were green beans, of course, probably picked that morning, cooked to perfection, and sliced hard-boiled eggs, tuna, onion and impossibly wonderful tomatoes, with a light vinaigrette to enhance every flavour. It was divine. And just like that, I knew how green beans should really taste.

I now love fresh green beans enough that I grow my own. It's not hard. About ten days after planting the seeds, the sturdy bowed stems break out of the soil like superheroes, pushing lumps and stones aside to straighten and reach toward the sun. A miracle to match "Jack and the Beanstalk." The bean seed at the top of each short stem then splits apart as two small, furled leaves appear. If the birds don't bite these tasty treats off, leaving pitiful headless stems behind, I know we will be eating delectable fresh beans in about five to six weeks. I grow bush varieties—knee-high leafy plants dripping with beans—and pole types such as the spectacular scarlet runner, climbing high above my head on a wooden teepee and covered in flame-red blossoms that turn into beans.

Wheat has been called the staff of life, but in reality, beans deserve the title. A source of protein for people the world over, they likely saved humanity from starvation countless times over thousands of years—in the form of dried beans shaped like tiny kidneys.

There are an enormous number of varieties, in a rainbow of colours and patterns. Harvested long after the bean plants have matured and dried in the fields, the inner seeds are removed from the tough pods. These dry, hard little seeds, or beans, as we call them, can be stored for months or even years. After soaking in water overnight and long cooking, these beans turn into a myriad of soups and stews.

In the Far East it was soy and mung beans, and in the Near East and around the Mediterranean it was favas, while in Africa it was cowpeas and black-eyed peas (actually beans), to name just a few. Nine thousand years ago, a different New World bean was growing in South America, most likely in Peru to start. These spread northward slowly into Mexico and Central America, up the east coast of North America and westward, as people shared seeds with one another. These beans were part of the famous Three Sisters cultivated by Native Americans: sprawling low squash plants to discourage weeds and shade the soil; maize or corn plants, which grew several feet high; and finally, bean plants that climbed and threaded their way up the cornstalks. A convenient, nutritious threesome.

When the Spanish arrived in the Americas, Columbus included, they noted that the beans were different from their own and took seeds back to Europe, where they joined European favas without much fuss or notice. History gets hazy here, and scientists are still making efforts to sort out names and genetics of the murky past of several thousand varieties of beans.

It didn't help that, at the time, dried beans were known as the poor man's meat and were generally ignored by the more fortunate, who preferred getting their protein in less flatulent forms—meat and fish. Dried beans have enjoyed a windy reputation, well deserved, since ancient times. The "musical fruit" indeed.

Things changed for beans when the Europeans, starting with the French, bred New World varieties to pick when they were unripe, green and tender. Enjoyed only in season, these were preferred by the upper classes—for taste and reduced "windiness." Today, we call them French beans, green beans, string beans, haricots verts or

Tender, fresh local beans, cooked to perfection, are equally wonderful served hot with butter or chilled and topped with snipped basil and a mild vinaigrette. Photo: Stratos Giannikos/Shutterstock.com

snap beans, and, strangely, wax beans when they are yellow. Thankfully, fresh beans are now eaten just about everywhere, by everyone, poor and rich alike.

These tender beans can be grown all over BC, and can be found in farmers' markets, piled high in heaps of green, purple and yellow, over several weeks, starting in late June. When buying, choose specimens that are firm, smooth and unblemished. Avoid pods bulging with large seeds, which have been picked past their prime. Refrigerate immediately and keep for a week or more. Before cooking, break off the end with the stem attached—which should make a snap sound if they are fresh. Keep those curly ends and leave beans whole. Steam, stir-fry or grill until barely tender.

I can sit down to a plate of just-cooked local green beans with butter and salt and believe I'm close to paradise. But to jazz things up a little, it's easy to make a salad that has stood the test of many summertime potlucks. First of all, buy a big bag of oh-so-fresh local beans at the market. Don't skimp; you'll be sorry if you do. Steam the beans—do not overcook—then quickly cool them in a colander under cold running water. Drain well and align the beans prettily on a bed of greens on your loveliest oval plate. Sprinkle snipped fresh basil across the middle. Pour your favourite vinaigrette over them and serve with tongs. Bask in all the praise sure to come from grateful diners, and make sure you get your share.

MR. ZUCCHINI AND FRIENDS

Zucchinis have a reputation for immoderation. In August, every gardener complains of an endless supply, which threatens to overwhelm cooks and diners with an abundance of the giant green dirigibles. By the end of the month, heaps of green boats appear at farm markets beside a sign saying "Free." I can never resist that kind of bargain, and since I am unable to abide wasting food especially of the locally grown, fresh variety—I head home with recipes dancing in my head.

It's strange to imagine, but not long ago, most North Americans had not heard of or seen zucchinis. I know my childhood was sadly lacking in this department. When it comes to vegetables, zucchinis are newcomers, a result of enthusiastic crossbreeding of squash in the countryside around Milan, Italy, in the late 1800s. The French later embraced them and, like the British, refer to them as courgettes, which makes them sound awfully posh. The Italians took their zucchini seeds with them when they emigrated in wave after wave to North America between 1880 and 1920. It took decades before the rest of us finally became fans of what was then called Italian squash. We seem to have made up for lost zuke time by growing and eating them with great enthusiasm ever since.

Other squashes have a more ancient pedigree. Native Americans first cultivated both summer and winter varieties in Central America and Mexico seven thousand years ago, and the easy-to-grow vegetables spread north and south to the rest of the Americas. In the fifteenth century, explorers like Columbus came across them growing everywhere. They took the seeds back to countries around the Mediterranean, where they were quickly adopted, especially by the Italians, who knew a good thing when they saw it.

Zucchinis are a member of the cucurbit or gourd family, an enormous and confusing bunch of vegetables that are actually botanically fruits. The clan includes summer squashes, winter squashes, cucumbers and melons. Summer squashes, such as zucchinis, are picked when they are young and immature, and the entire vegetable—skin, flesh and seeds—is tender and edible. Winter squashes, such as butternuts, acorns and pumpkins, are left to grow on the vine for another month or two so they develop tough skins and large, hard seeds inside. Unlike tender squashes, they store well for months.

Summer squashes such as zucchinis are picked as youngsters so that their skin, innards and seeds are soft and edible, unlike tough mature winter squashes. Photo: AJCespedes/Shutterstock.com

Italian immigrants brought their favourite summer squash seeds with them to North America around 1900—but the rest of us were slow to discover them. Photo: Ivana Lalicki/Shutterstock.com

There are now over three hundred varieties of summer squashes grown in North America. That means we can expect different and interesting types to show up at the farmers' market. The main groups include the petite, flying saucer–shaped scallops or pattypans—surely the cutest name in the veggie world—and zucchinis. Then there are vegetable marrows, crooknecks, straightnecks and cocozelles—but these labels are somewhat fluid in the squash world. Shapes vary from the narrow, curling Tromboncino, which grows up to 150 centimetres long, to the round eight-ball zukes, and colours range from yellow to green to pale white, with striped and even two-tone varieties. Though many summer squashes are smooth skinned, the yellow crookneck is warty, and the Italian heirloom Romanesco is ridged.

Exotics include the Miriam sponge gourd, which tastes like zucchini when young and tender. If left on the vine to grow to adult size, it eventually dries completely inside and out—and I mean downright parched—and the skin flakes off to reveal…you'd never guess…a loofah within. A vegetable good for eating or exfoliating—isn't Mother Nature full of surprises?

Summer squash grows all over BC, but frost at either end of the season is deadly. The plants adore sun and heat, and though they need regular drinks, they don't really care for rain on their big leaves. They are often planted on "hills" or small mounds, which allows the vines to trail all over the ground in opposite directions. Every plant is bisexual—monoecious is the correct term—and has male and female flowers. Bees carry pollen from the former to the latter, and a mere few days later, a squash is ready to pick. When more than one kind of squash is grown in the same veggie patch, bees happily dance from one plant to another to pollinate different varieties, sometimes producing veggies harbouring new and unique mystery seeds—nature's own crossbreeding program.

We can look forward to the first BC summer squash harvests, most often small zucchinis, in late June. The bounty continues to increase—and increase—until the first frost comes along, usually in October. When buying, look for firm specimens with a sheen, which fades if the veggie has spent too much time in the field. Smaller is better—zucchinis get fibrous and airy when oversized. Thin-skinned summer squash is easily nicked, even with a fingernail, and does not travel well—a good reason to buy directly from the farmer at markets or roadside stands, in season. Store all summer squash in the fridge and use within a week.

In the kitchen, summer squash is wonderfully adaptable, and any type can be used in any dish. We can enjoy it raw as crudités with a dip, or grated into a myriad of dishes, like omelettes, frittatas, pancakes, quick breads and cookies. When cooked on its own, it should be stir-fried, sautéed or barbecued, as it tends to get mushy when boiled or stewed because of its high water content.

I am a true summer squash lover and adore the smooth, mild, comforting taste when it's barely cooked. I can easily devour an entire zucchini sliced, brushed with marinade and braised on the

Over 300 varieties of summer squash are grown in North America, which means we can expect to find unusual shapes, sizes and colours at the farmers' market. Photo: Nanna_Kirkegaard/Shutterstock.com

barbecue, both sides, until just tender. A few years ago, in a very expensive restaurant in Provence, we were served a side dish of heaven. The closest I have come to repeating the experience is to fry up a medium-sized grated zucchini in butter on medium high for a couple of minutes, then add one-quarter cup of milk to sizzle for a minute or so until the milk is absorbed. I top with grated Parmesan. Summer squash, revealed.

But my all-time favourite way to cook with zucchini is rata-touille, which uses a medley of BC's late-summer vegetables grown to perfection in the hot August sun. Cut one small eggplant and one zucchini into pieces the size of cherry tomatoes and put into

Most summer squashes, no matter the variety, size, shape or colour, are interchangeable in sweet or savoury recipes. Photo: Caroline Attwood/Unsplash

a saucepan. Add one large onion and a green pepper, each cut into stamp-sized pieces, plus one large garlic clove, smashed, though garlic lovers may prefer to add more, much more. Select four big, beautiful, ripe tomatoes and remove the skins by first immersing in boiling water for a few seconds. Then remove and peel—the skin will come off easily. Chop and add to the rest. Bring the combo to a slight boil, then turn down to a simmer. Give it a stir occasionally. Though it doesn't look promising to start, this mélange will turn into a thick, creamy dish after one hour of burbling away. Ratatouille can be enjoyed as a casserole topped with cheese melted in the oven, or as a side dish served hot or at room temperature. A hearty, nourishing and delicious way to celebrate the cream of BC's crop as the growing season comes to an end.

BRING ON THE BROCCOLI—AND THE CAULIFLOWER TOO

In the beginning there was only cabbage. It took old-fashioned human creativity, patience and persistence to bring us cauliflower and broccoli, bred from low-lying, loose-leafed cabbage plants growing in the wild. It was likely the ancient peoples of Northern Italy, known for their ingenuity in the garden, who selected and cross-bred wild plants over generations to develop tiny cabbage flowers into large, edible heads on top of thick stalks. And voila—there was broccoli. The origins of cauliflower are murkier, but tinkering with cabbage also produced a different sort of head with tightly packed, unopened flowers on a short stem—behold the cauliflower. Mark Twain famously declared that cauliflower was "nothing better than a cabbage with a college education." Now there was a man who knew his vegetables.

The ancient Romans held broccoli and cauliflower in high regard. Emperor Tiberius apparently had a fetish: for one month he insisted on eating only broccoli until his father told him to smarten up. After leading a quiet life during the Middle Ages, both vegetables made a splash again in Europe by the 1500s. Catherine de' Medici brought broccoli to France with her when she married Henry II in 1533. And King Louis XIV of France, a foodie extraordinaire, embraced both veggies with enthusiasm during the late 1600s. Madame du Barry, Louis XV's mistress, was so enamoured with cauliflower that cream soups and side dishes still bear her name. Or it may be that the white vegetable and soup reminded people of her pale skin and powdered

Opposite: Madame du Barry, mistress of King Louis XV of France, lent her name to white cauliflower soups and side dishes, possibly due to her pale powdered hairdo. Photo: Jennifer Schmidt/Unsplash

hairdo, but we'll never know for sure. Both vegetables remained a rare luxury in Europe until the 1800s, when they became widely cultivated—for the common people.

After the vegetables arrived in England, the British took them to India in the early 1800s, where they are still staples. China now grows the most broccoli and cauliflower, followed by India. North Americans were slow adopters until Italian immigrants cultivated and shipped large quantities from California to the East Coast in the 1920s. It seems all of us in the North and East have been eating California broccoli for almost one hundred years.

In spite of decades of overcooking (mush, anyone?)—and George W. Bush's declaration that, as president, he wasn't going to eat any more broccoli, so there!—cauliflower and broccoli are enjoying a renaissance in popularity. Both are nutritional powerhouses. My mother, an early fan of wholesome eating, insisted on serving only colourful dark green and crimson veggies, but she was wrong about pale cauliflower—it packs a healthful punch too.

White cauliflower may become part of history as we return to a choice of colours that were common hundreds of years ago. In 1970, a small orange cauliflower was discovered growing all alone in a field of white specimens outside Toronto. It was a mutant, a rare genetic accident. The little oddball was shipped to Cornell University in New York State, where scientists worked for decades, crossbreeding it with white cauliflower (no GMO meddling), to produce orange varieties like Cheddar and Sunset, suitable for cultivation and full of beta carotene. Purple varieties like Graffiti and Purple Cape are now hitting markets and contain healthful anthocyanin, also found in purple cabbage and red wine. In 1988, an American seed company perfected broccoflower—an attractive, green-coloured broccoli-cauliflower cross originally grown in the Netherlands. These veggies look like a painter's palette on the appetizer plate, and they are good for us too.

Broccoli is experiencing a redo as well. In the 1990s the Sakura Seed Corporation in Japan crossed ordinary broccoli with gai lan, a

Chinese broccoli (also called Chinese kale), to bring us broccolini (sometimes known as baby broccoli). With smaller, looser heads than regular broccoli, and thin stems similar to asparagus, the entire vegetable is tender and edible: leaves, stems and flowers. Rapini, also known as broccoli rabe or raab, causes some confusion. It looks like a leafier cousin of broccolini, but it actually belongs to the turnip, not cabbage, family. Another broccolini look-alike—a purple sprouting variety—overwinters in southern BC, shooting up in late winter and early spring—a bonus!

Broccoli and cauliflower are cousins, both bred over centuries from cabbage ancestors to produce tight little flower buds on thick short stalks. Photo: Delaney Zayac, Ice Cap Organics, Pemberton, BC

Though it looks like a futuristic cauliflower for aliens, the beautiful Romanesco is a type of broccoli that has been grown in Italy for hundreds of years. Photo: Nazzu/ Shutterstock.com

The exotic Romanesco broccoli, in fashionable chartreuse, looks and tastes more like a cauliflower. It is an Italian heirloom—some say from the sixteenth century—with unusual conical peaks swirling in a spiral around its tightly packed head. Looking more like a science fiction vegetable than real food, the Romanesco made a cameo appearance in the film *Star Wars: The Force Awakens* as an alien, futuristic, outer-space veggie.

Both broccoli and cauliflower are cool-weather vegetables and grow well in BC. Planted in the spring, they take two to three months to mature before they are cut off close to the ground. Baby broccoli shows up earlier, but most of the harvest starts in earnest by July and continues until the end of September or later. With common broccoli, look for tight flowers in packed heads and firm stems with freshly cut ends. Avoid any with flowers that have bloomed into yellow, making the heads bitter. Store in the fridge, bagged, for up to a week. With cauliflower, search for heavy, dense heads without brown spots or patches. When bagged, it will last for at least two weeks or longer in the fridge.

It's easy to freeze broccoli to eat all winter. I like to buy a supply at my favourite Richmond farmers' market. I am never happier than when I am there, rolling my cart around on uneven, puddle-dotted asphalt between giant cardboard and wooden boxes heaped with locally grown bounty. Although I know that this market imports some things, it makes every effort to offer BC fruit from the Okanagan and vegetables from the Lower Mainland. It's always crowded, and I love to see what other customers, speaking a myriad of languages, put in their buggies. The cauliflowers are giants and still have their long, stiff leaves curling around their heads, which hide them from the sun. I snap this greenery off to fit them into my cart. Broccoli beckons, piled high and harvested that morning, with a sign saying "Our Local Broccoli" in black marker—meaning it comes from the field out back, just like the cauliflower.

I tend to fill my stand-alone freezer with a winter supply of frozen produce, but small-scale freezing works just as well. Buy a double batch of locally grown broccoli—some for dinner and some for the freezer. Remove tough stems and cut heads into equal-sized pieces. Blanch by plunging into boiling water for three minutes, then pour into a colander in the sink under cold running water. Add ice cubes to cool everything down immediately. Drain and spread on towels to dry. Then spread on cookie sheets to freeze before bagging. While not suitable for raw eating or stir-fries, frozen broccoli works for just about everything else, and it's justifiable to feel proud when pulling it out of the freezer in January. Make that one for BC, one less for California.

Broccoli and cauliflower have branched out in the kitchen. Once limited to soggy vegetable sides or dull veggies and dip, we now slice them raw into salads, steam, stir-fry, bake and roast them, and incorporate them into curries, quiches, omelettes and pastas. Conveniently, these two veggies can usually be substituted one for the other or, even better, used in combination.

One of my favourite broccoli and cauliflower dishes is a cream soup. I come from the use-whatever-is-in-the-fridge school of soup making, which means my results are different every time. But one thing is a given: my soups always begin with sautéing one chopped onion and smashed garlic (one clove or more) in olive oil till translucent. For this soup, add one stalk of celery in there too. If time is short, skip the sautéing part. Next, add about three cups of chicken or vegetable broth. Of course, the real thing is best, but bouillon cubes or powder will do in a pinch. Prepare about four cups of broccoli and/or cauliflower pieces. No need to discard tough broccoli stems—just peel, chop and use them as well. Not enough veggies? Grate a carrot and/or a potato to add to the mix. Throw all the vegetables into the pot, bring to a boil and simmer until everything is fork tender. No crispy veggies allowed here. Purée the soup in portions, using a blender or food processor until coarsely creamy, and pour each batch into a second pot. Stir in one tablespoon of fancy mustard (grainy, Dijon or whatever is in the fridge) and three-quarter cup of grated cheddar, the older the better. Add water if the soup is too thick and bring almost to a boil. Serve topped with a sprinkle of grated cheddar to look like a pro.

Not quite à la du Barry, but just as delicious, and healthier too.

COOL AS A CUCUMBER

I have a small greenhouse in my backyard that I use to grow cucumbers. I carefully transplant the seedlings I've started from seed into old five-gallon buckets lining the walls. They look ridiculously small and precious in their giant pots. Most cucumbers are climbers, and once they hit their stride, the thick, moist stems grow inches in days while sending out long tendrils reaching for something, anything to

Cucumbers are heat lovers and thrive in greenhouses or out in the hot BC summer sunshine, their vines reaching out to climb or trail for several feet. Photo: iStock.com/Garsya

grab. I tie knee-high plants to wooden supports embedded in the pails. I manipulate sticky runners and wrestle with shooting stalks, attempting to attach them to a network of strings fixed to the rafters above. The cucumber leaves flourish to become large and plentiful, hanging like pointy green umbrellas over yellow blossoms. Despite my best efforts to be the boss, nature rules as the cucumbers grow into a jungle, one plant winding its way through the next, a wall of green. Blossoms, instantly it seems, turn into cucumbers, surprising me day after day. "Oh! Where did *you* come from?" I mutter to the newcomer peeping out from under the foliage. It's the thrill of the hunt as I peer under the leaves, inspect overhead runaways and examine the vines trailing rebelliously along the floor and behind the containers. Each plant produces between five and twenty cucumbers. I never find them all.

Because cucumbers are tender and touchy and cannot deal with frosts, they must be started as seedlings inside or seeded outside in June when the soil is toasty. The plants are demanding too, insisting on lots of space, plenty of nourishment, copious amounts of water and abundant heat and sunshine—the whole shebang. Cucumbers can be grown in the field or inside a greenhouse, and fresh annual harvests show up in BC farmers' markets, roadside stands and grocery stores in July, August and September.

At one time, the only type of cucumber available in most of North America was regular (also called slicing or field) cukes, with many large seeds running down the centre and thick, dark green skin requiring peeling or scoring with a fork. These days, we've moved well beyond these stalwarts.

English cucumbers, introduced to North America in the 1970s, were hailed as burpless—a distinct advantage over their gassier slicing cousins. These thin-skinned, long, slender and almost seedless cucumbers are grown in the field during summer, but also in BC greenhouses nearly all year round. Nubbly pale green Asian cukes and petite, intensely green Japanese and Persian types have joined the seedless and politely burpless pack.

Pickling cucumbers, sometimes called dill cukes, are stubby, spiny miniatures and include the tiny gherkin—*cornichons* to the French. These midgets can be eaten raw and unpeeled, but most head into the pickle jar.

Exotics like Armenian, or snake, cucumbers are sweet, tender and soft-seeded but are actually more of a melon—a cucumber relative. Baseball-shaped yellow lemon cukes, an Australian heirloom, round out our selection—though market farmers continue to delight and surprise us with new choices.

Cucumbers weren't always crisp, juicy or even tasty. They started out in the wild—small, tough and dry— probably in India. First cultivated and improved by breeding at least three thousand years ago, they made their way east and west, where they were enthusiastically embraced by the ancient Egyptians, Greeks and Chinese. The Romans liked them even more; almost two thousand years ago Emperor Tiberius insisted on eating them every day, all year. In summer, his minions grew them in wheeled carts they rolled around to catch the strongest rays of the sun, and in winter, cucumbers were grown for him in what were probably the first greenhouses, covered with thin slices of translucent mica rock.

In spite of these initial successes, cucumbers have had their ups and downs. After being brought by the Romans to Europe, where King Charlemagne of the Franks insisted on having them in his royal garden in the eighth century, they almost disappeared through war, plague and neglect before being resurrected again in the 1400s. Columbus took seeds to Haiti in 1494, and immigrants brought them to the east coast of North America. Indigenous populations happily added them to their gardens of squash, beans and corn all the way from Florida to Quebec. Jacques Cartier discovered them growing near Montreal when he landed there in 1535. However, in the 1600s, physicians foolishly decided that eating them raw was unhealthy, even dangerous, and warned against it in medical journals. In August—cucumber season—1663, Englishman Samuel Pepys wrote in his diary that two acquaintances had died after eating them. For a

Dill cukes, small and spiny, are traditionally grown to be pickled—so we can enjoy their crunchy flavour all winter long. Photo: Viktor Byvshev/Shutterstock.com

while, cukes were persona non grata in western Europe and North America. But they beat this dire reputation to rise again by the time Victoria reigned in England. Think cucumber tea sandwiches.

Cucumbers pack light nutritional clout compared with other fruits and vegetables. At 95 percent water, consider them more of a drink—a green water bottle. And "cool as a cucumber" is more than an expression; the vegetables are eleven degrees Celsius colder inside than out. Their timing—appearing ripe and ready during the hottest months—is perfect.

When buying fresh in-season cukes—always the tastiest— choose firm specimens without blemishes or wrinkles. They should feel heavy (that's juicy) for their size. Smaller ones will likely be more flavourful. Store in the fridge, bagged if possible, and do not wash until just before eating. Don't let them languish—enjoy without delay.

My favourite way to savour the summer's bounty is in tzatziki. I can never get enough and it couldn't be easier to make. I add finely chopped cucumber to yogurt and stir—a delicious accompaniment to flatbread, barbecued skewers or curries. But it's impossible to think about cucumbers without considering pickles. Fermenting in either brine or vinegar has been with us since ancient days as a way to keep them long after the harvest is over.

Traditional methods are many and varied—and often time-consuming. To keep things simple and avoid spoilage and canning dangers like botulism, I now prefer refrigerator pickles. I can use my excess harvest to quickly make up a jar or two of crunchy bread-and-butter pickles that are ready to eat within a week. It's a perfect way to take advantage of locally grown cucumbers heaped high in markets during our hottest days. Any variety or mix of cucumber can be used, from small dills to long English cukes. If using tougher-skinned field types, score skins with a fork or peel.

Wash 10 dill-sized cukes, or equivalent, and slice thinly. Add 1 small onion and 1 pepper of any colour, also thinly sliced. Make sure you have enough to snugly fill two 1-litre Mason jars (or four 500-millilitre jars), then put in a bowl. In a saucepan, combine 1½ cups white vinegar, 3 cups sugar, 1½ tablespoons pickling or kosher salt, ¾ teaspoon each of celery seed and mustard powder and a heaping ¼ teaspoon turmeric. Bring to a boil to dissolve, simmer for 5 minutes and pour over the cucumber mixture. Let cool, cover and refrigerate for 4 days. Stir occasionally to make sure the vegetables are immersed in liquid. Transfer veggies into Mason jars that have been sterilized by spending 10 minutes in a 225-degree-Fahrenheit oven, then fill to top with brine and refrigerate. Voila—they are ready to eat. Most of the pickling liquid (and sugar) will be left behind as you snack on these crisp and flavourful pickles. They'll keep for a month in the fridge—if they last that long.

PEACHY KEEN

The woman standing next to me in the produce section reached over, chose a peach and brought it close to her face. "Oh, the smell of these," she sighed, as she took another, weighing it in her hand. "I have a peach tree at home, on the Island." Oh, the envy.

For the first part of my life, I lived in places far removed from fresh produce of any kind. Back then, fruits and vegetables took days longer to get anywhere, jostled in the backs of trucks for a week. The only peaches I met with were canned. I tried to appreciate them the way Laura Ingalls Wilder did in *By the Shores of Silver Lake*, licking every drop of the "sweet golden juice" off her spoon, but they never did much for me.

It was when I ended up in BC—Lotus Land, they called it then—that my peach love affair began. One August, my roommate, Lynn, and I set out on a road trip to check in on friends and acquaintances scattered around the province. She was BC born and bred, but it was all new territory to me. Our first stop was Kamloops, where we bunked in with a mutual chum, right in the middle of peach season.

Seated at the kitchen table with a bowl of fresh peaches in the centre, Lynn demonstrated exactly how to eat a fresh peach. It was a ritual involving a paring knife, a plate and a perfect-as-you-can-find peach. First, peel the peach. The fuzzy skin peels away easily from a ripe specimen. Then cut the peach into slices like one of those Christmas chocolate oranges, one at a time, sliding each delectable

Opposite: Varieties like Redhaven, Fairhaven, Glohaven, Cresthaven and O'Henry ripen one after another, meaning that we can savour BC peaches from the middle of July until September. Photo: Sea Wave/Shutterstock.com

Enthusiasm for growing peaches set off a real estate boom in the Okanagan Valley in 1897, but success was elusive for orchardists. Photo: Ian Baldwin/Unsplash

piece off the knife and into your mouth as you cut them. Choose another peach and repeat. Wipe chin when necessary. That first time, I ate four, because I really had no idea peaches tasted like that.

Peaches, fuzzless nectarines and their close cousins, apricots, are the most tender tree fruits grown in our province. Cherries, plums and apples are tougher. While peach trees can withstand and even need winter freezing spells, a late cold snap can kill the spring blossoms that turn into fruits. Peaches adore summer heat and sun but require regular watering—which means the Okanagan is perfect, with irrigation.

Enthusiasm for fruit growing in the Okanagan Valley set off a real estate boom starting in 1897—with aptly named Peachland. By 1900, the valley was host to over one million fruit trees. However, things were rocky as farmers had trouble getting their fruits to customers; peaches in particular had to be transported gently. It wasn't until 1914, when the Kettle Valley Railway was finally completed, that fruit could catch a smooth ride all the way from the Kootenays through the Okanagan Valley and down to the coast.

Today, BC grows a large crop of peaches, almost six tons, in the semi-arid, hot south—the Okanagan, Similkameen and Creston Valleys—along with smaller harvests on Vancouver Island and in the Fraser Valley. Almost all are sold for fresh eating, showing up at roadside stands, farmers' markets and grocery stores.

Over the years, I've heard many people toss out peach names—most commonly Redhaven and cling-free—usually incorrectly. I learned the truth about different types when, one hot-as-heck day in the Okanagan, my husband and I swung off the beaten track onto a back road, following "Fresh Peaches" thataway signs. We ended up in a giant barn, the smell of peaches heavy in the sultry, still air, surrounded by crates heaped with them in a wide variety of colours and sizes—more than I had ever seen in one place before.

A woman who looked like she'd picked a peach or two sat perched on a stool as we made the rounds, perusing our choices. We asked what was what, and that's how I found out that the very first and the very best BC peaches—at least for my taste—are Early Redhavens, small with firm smooth flesh, both tart and sweet, with the delicate aftertaste of sunshine.

Next up are plain Redhavens—slightly larger, still to die for—and then a whole litany of names I had never heard of, like Fairhaven, Glohaven, Cresthaven and O'Henry, among others. These varieties ripen one after another, meaning that we can savour BC peaches from the middle of July until September if the weather co-operates.

Cling-free, or freestone, peaches aren't a variety at all, but refer to those that are slightly easier to remove from the pit in halves.

Cling peaches, like Redhavens, hold on to that rough, almond-like centre a little harder—not at all a concern for fresh eating, especially one slice at a time.

It is a wonder of modern commerce that local peaches, in season, sit beside the California jobs, which seem to show up for months and months. Apparently, this trend to produce hard, travel-worthy fruit has resulted in people who actually prefer their peaches "crispy," more like an apple. No chance of juice dribbling down your chin with those. No chance of them tasting like real peaches either.

BC peaches are picked when almost ripe to help them travel, but they continue to ripen off the tree. Happily, my local grocery store proudly stocks them. As soon as the first ones appear, I buy them every few days, choosing carefully—no bruises or dents—and gently fill a bag or two. At the till, I become freakishly possessive, as I insist on moving my precious purchase across the scale myself. If I can, I buy a box at the farmers' market to increase my booty. At home, I lay out dinner plates and sort the peaches according to ripeness, gently pressing down on one end to test for softness and looking for a greenish cast. My kitchen and dining room are a sea of peaches: those to eat now, those to eat in a couple of days and those to eat in a week. They are my babies. Only if our eating does not keep up do my peaches see the inside of the fridge to halt ripening.

In the mornings, we love pancakes and peaches. To make this scrumptious breakfast, drop one egg in a bowl, add one cup of white flour and one-half cup of whole wheat flour. Add enough milk to make a thin batter when whisked. Cook in a well-buttered frying pan; it doesn't take long. Meantime, slice some ripe peaches as described above, and add a small amount of slightly warmed maple syrup to prevent browning. Top a stack of pancakes with this heavenly mixture. I store leftover pancakes in the fridge because I know we'll want this treat again tomorrow, and the next day, and the day after that.

Sometimes I try to freeze some of the peach harvest. I gently toss slices with lemon juice, freeze them on parchment-covered

Fuzzless nectarines and flavourful apricots are kissing cousins of peaches that also thrive in the hot sunny valleys of southern British Columbia. Photo: LUM3N/Unsplash

cookie sheets, then bag them for mid-winter smoothies, but it's really, really hard to go through the peach ritual and miss the putting-it-in-your-mouth part. Each year, we work our way through twenty-five kilograms, or more if our offspring appear, gorging ourselves so that the taste memory of the divine peach season stays with us long after it is over, which is always much too soon.

PETER PICKED A PEPPER

My husband and I have long-time friends who have lived in the Okanagan Valley for years. They are the most contented, down-to-earth people we know. In their backyard, they tend a small vegetable patch, but they also take full advantage of the cornucopia of fruits and vegetables that are grown around them. They know about all the nearby farm markets, where to buy the best peaches, when the U-picks are open and how to find the best wine.

We visited them in late August last year—right at harvest time. They took us to a local winery where we tasted and tested before heading down into the vineyard to eat the picnic lunch we'd brought—with a bottle of white, of course. We chose a table set at the edge of the grass, so close to the grapevines we could almost touch them. The winery supplied a basket with blue-checked cloth napkins and cutlery nestled inside. Charming. We chatted, voices hushed, silverware softly clinking in the outdoors, feeling like we were somewhere in France. The air was warm and soft as it often is in the Okanagan. Peaceful and perfect.

Then we headed off for a more purposeful task—a visit to a U-pick for peppers. We stopped in at the gate to pick up giant five-gallon buckets, two each. They were smudged with farm dirt inside and out. This was serious, sizable pepper picking. We were directed out to the field, the pails knocking against our legs as we walked single file in the fading afternoon sunshine. The plants nudged close to each other in rows and came up above our knees. Our footsteps were soft in the silky fine soil, which was dusty dry

Opposite: Columbus thought he had hit the pepper jackpot in the New World when he discovered chili peppers—and erroneously named them after peppercorns. Photo: Sergei Leto/Shutterstock.com

from the heat of the day. There were peppers everywhere: littered on the ground and hanging, hidden under the leaves, from every bush. I'd never seen anything like it. Stripey purple, pale yellow, intense green and brilliant red, all cone shaped, all impressively large. It was just too easy, and we each filled our first bucket within minutes. People picking plentiful peppers—our own tongue twister. We decided to get choosier with the second pail, reaching out for only the most perfect of the crop. Within thirty minutes, we were headed back to pay for our bonanza, adding boxes of plum tomatoes from the same farm to our harvest. Visions of homemade salsa and pasta sauce danced in our heads as we loaded up the car. A day later, my husband and I headed home, grateful for the bounty and friendship we always find in the Okanagan Valley.

The peppers we picked that afternoon were mild and are called bell or sweet peppers. Chili peppers, cousins from the same plant family, pack a spicier bite. Both types were probably cultivated six thousand years ago in Central and South America. In 1492, Columbus came poking around, looking for another spice route to Asia. When he came across chili peppers, he thought he had hit the jackpot. He figured these piquant delights could replace peppercorns, which at the time were worth their weight in gold and available only from India and Southeast Asia. In his excitement, he named this new plant discovery pepper too—a misnomer we have been stuck with ever since.

Columbus took chili pepper seeds back to Europe, and within a mere fifty years, the Portuguese and Spanish shared them with Italy, North Africa, India and China. Their rapid spread was a testament to humanity's enthusiasm for spicy heat, which has remained undimmed ever since. Hundreds of types of chili peppers are grown today, varying in heat, or pungency, the official term, due to differing concentrations of the chemical capsaicin. In 1912, American pharmacist Wilbur Scoville invented a method of measuring the spiciness of different chili peppers by a taste test using a series of pepper dilutions. The Scoville scale, measured in Scoville heat units

Nutritious as well as delicious, mild sweet peppers, especially reds, can contain two to four times as much vitamin C as an orange. Photo: Brent Hofacker/Shutterstock. com

(SHU), is still in use today. Green bell peppers register at 0, ja-lapenos at 3,500–10,000 SHU, cayennes at 30,000–50,000 SHU and habaneros at 100,000–350,000 SHU. The hottest peppers in the world register in the millions—downright dangerous. That's why capsaicin is used in pepper sprays for bears and elephants.

Mild bell peppers made much less of a splash, but they did make their way around the world by the 1800s. Better late than never. Delicious raw, stewed, stir-fried, roasted and pickled, they are nutritious as well; each pepper contains two to four times as much vitamin C as an orange.

Pepper plants love sunshine and hot weather and can't abide frosts. In BC, seedlings are started inside, then planted in the field

Fresh local BC peppers, plentiful in late summer, can easily be chopped and then frozen to add to sauces or pizza for a hint of sunshine all winter long. Photo: Bonnie Kittle/Unsplash

when it's balmy. After they've basked in the heat of the summer, harvesting of field bell peppers starts in July and extends until Jack Frost visits. Green peppers are usually less expensive because they are actually immature. If left on the bush, they slowly turn yellow, then orange, then red. As they ripen, they get sweeter and the vitamin C content increases. You get what you pay for.

When buying in season, watch for field peppers that tend to be a little lopsided and less perfectly shaped—that means they're local. Farmers at markets often offer unusual varieties in fun shapes and colours. I like the butter-coloured pointy Hungarian sort. Peppers should be glossy, without blemishes, soft spots or wrinkles, and firm if thick-skinned. They can be stored in bags in the fridge for a week or two.

My haul of peppers from the Okanagan provided plenty of fresh eating, but I froze some as well. I diced an assortment of coloured peppers, spread them on cookie sheets to freeze and then bagged them to add to sauces all winter. Next, I made salsa. Being a little lazy, I tend to lean toward freezing rather than canning—no worries about acidity, no standing over a boiling kettle. I'm careful not to overfill, and I leave the lids off the jars until after the salsa is frozen. There is nothing like a little jar of Okanagan sunshine in deepest, darkest winter.

But fresh is best, and I like to make my corn and pepper salad to bring out the flavours of BC's August bounty. To make this colourful dish, rinse a 540-millilitre can of black beans, drain well and put in a bowl. Cook 3 cobs of sweet BC corn in boiling water for 4 minutes, then cool slightly. Slice the kernels off and add to beans. Last night's leftover corn is fine if it has been wrapped and refrigerated. Add 1 diced red pepper. Snip Italian parsley (regular will do in a pinch) with scissors into pieces over salad—this is tedious so keep at it till you are bored (that should be enough). For dressing, combine 3 tablespoons olive oil, 1½ tablespoons cider vinegar, 3 teaspoons honey and the juice of ¾ of a lime. Mix dressing thoroughly and add to the salad. Toss. Serve right away or, even better, marinate for a few hours in the fridge. Perfect for a summer potluck or family dinner on the deck and almost too pretty to eat.

THE PRIVATE LIFE OF CORN

During August and September, I should really have a sign in my rear-view window that says "Stops Suddenly for Corn." I'm constantly scanning roadside pullouts and empty lots, watching for beat-up trucks and vans marooned in odd places. When I spot the words "Chilliwack Corn" scrawled on dusty cardboard or weathered ply-wood, my car veers in like a homing pigeon.

The sweetest, juiciest, pop-in-your-mouth cobs I have ever found were in Burnaby, on Kingsway, of all places. Mired in rush-hour traffic, I noticed a pale blue pickup parked on a corner lot where a gas station had met its maker. Two scruffy young fellows, clad in plaid shirts and faded jeans, sat on the tailgate, dangling their legs and smoking, not a care in the world on a warm and golden afternoon. They had pushed their entire load of corn out onto the gravel, where it sat in a heap. No sign, just the corn itself in a pile. Standing on my brakes, I took the plunge and swerved in, my car bouncing over uneven ground. I climbed out and slowly circled the mound, then inspected a couple of cobs, peeling back a husk or two. The corn was perfect. Plump, even, medium-sized kernels, moist tassels and green husks. Freshly picked this morning in Chilliwack, they said.

Next came the inevitable thorny question: how many to buy. Six, twelve, perhaps more? I paced. I dithered. I can munch my way through up to five consecutive stellar-tasting cobs. On the other hand, if the corn does not meet my high standards, I won't even finish one. I'd had enough of the dry, chewy, starchy stuff to last a lifetime when I lived far away from anything that could be called remotely fresh. In the end I took a dozen of that Kingsway corn to dinner with some friends, and they found it hilarious when I politely restricted myself to four.

It is a marvel that corn—properly called maize—even grows cobs. The sex life of corn is so outlandish that only nature, in all her wisdom, could have conceived it. Each cob-to-be (the girl part) is covered with rows of tiny flowers: four hundred to eight hundred of them, all wrapped up tightly in the husk, playing hard to get. The tassel at the top of the stalk (the boy part) produces fourteen to eighteen million grains of powdery yellow pollen over a few days when the time is right. Each one of those flowers has to be fertilized by one of those grains to produce a kernel, but not to worry—each girl (flower) puts out a sticky strand of silk to lure in one of the twenty thousand grains available for every one of them. When a grain of pollen gets lucky and lands on a silk strand, it splits in two, the first half tunnelling down the silk to make way for the second half to follow and fertilize the flower. The industrious first half then joins in the fun, and bingo! All is set for the metamorphosis from flower into kernel. A special threesome for each and every kernel—think of that the next time you bite into a cob.

The sex life of corn—involving thousands of boy and girl parts—is so outlandish that only a mischievous Mother Nature with a sense of humour could have conceived it. Photo: Oksana Shevchenko/Shutterstock.com

Botanists call corn a "hopeless monster"—strong words for a plant. But they have their reasons. Firstly, corn would vanish without us. Left to their own devices, corncobs, overfull of tightly wrapped, imprisoned seeds (kernels), fall to the ground and sit, like helpless mummies. If the kernels do manage to escape, masses of seedlings sprout all at once, crowding and overwhelming each other on one tiny bit of earth. Human hands (or machines operated by them) are needed to harvest the kernels and plant them as seeds, spaced to allow each plant to grow. For nine thousand years, people and corn have existed together in this mutually beneficial relationship.

Which begs another question: Where did corn come from in the first place? Until recently, nothing remotely resembling corn, a strange type of grass with tall, ramrod-straight stalks, narrow, three-foot leaves and peculiar cobs, could be found in the wild. Scientists spent lifetimes trying to solve the mystery of corn. Mayans quite reasonably thought it came from the Maize God. Finally, a vaguely corn-like grass called teosinte was discovered in Mexico in 1978. Eventually, genetic testing confirmed teosinte is a distant relative that, through a natural mutation thousands of years ago, set up humans as corn eaters and cultivators.

Corn is the largest and most important grain crop grown in the world, providing a major food source when mature tough kernels are ground. Think tortillas, corn rotis, polenta and cornbread. Corn is easy to cross-pollinate, and we have inherited thousands of varieties of maize that grow in different soils and climates. Corn has been bred for popping (popcorn was eaten like cereal with milk and maple syrup in the 1700s), silage (fodder for livestock, especially pigs, which eat cobs, stalks, leaves and all), biofuel (for ethanol), oils (corn oil), food additives (corn syrup and cornstarch) and just plain additives (in crayons, fabrics, soap, plastics, lipstick and fireworks, to name merely a few).

Opposite: People can be particular about how they cook their corn—but it's always worth the hunt to find the freshest locally grown corn available. Photo: Dragne Marius/Unsplash

Only 1 percent of the worldwide maize crop is grown as sweet corn for us to eat off the cob, fresh and immature (or "green"), as a vegetable. In BC, it is mostly grown in the Lower Mainland and South Coast region, in the Okanagan Valley and on Vancouver Island. The window for picking perfect sweet corn, all harvested by hand, is small: four to five days. Too early and the kernels are small; too late and the sweetness is lost. Varieties with delicious names like Honeysweet, Ambrosia, Sugar Buns and Kandy Korn mature at different times, extending the season from the end of a hot July through the chill days of October.

An old saying claims that the best way to cook corn is to put the water on to boil and then go out and cut the ears, which is all very well if you have a field out back you are farming. Some—that would be farmers—say raw corn eaten right in the field is best. The rest of us are left to hunt and hope for the freshest we can find. At the market, roadside or supermarket, ask where the corn came from, and when. It doesn't pay to be shy when it comes to corn. Take it home and refrigerate immediately, in the husks or in plastic bags if naked, to slow the conversion of sugar to starch. Then eat it that night for dinner.

People tend to get tetchy about how to cook corn. My husband is a three-minute man, while I slide toward four. Some don't cook it at all, or barely. Barbecued corn is second to none. Each to his own.

Being the corn fan I am, it's hard for me to do anything but eat all the cobs straight from the pot, slathered with butter and generously salted. I dig in with both hands—none of those dainty little plastic miniature cobs with two spikes on the end to make it more ladylike for me. However, should the number of cooked cobs outnumber the appetites on hand, I happily wrap and refrigerate leftover cobs. The next day, I slice off the kernels to add to a salad—a sweet addition almost like candy. During corn season, I make sure to buy plenty and eat often because, as Garrison Keillor says, "sex is good, but not as good as fresh sweet corn."

Tomato Tales

When it comes to tomatoes, people tend to fall into two different camps. There are those who, while claiming they like tomatoes, actually prefer thin, pale slices on their burgers or chewy cherry-sized versions in salads. Bona fide tomato lovers, on the other hand, think a piece of heaven can be found by biting straight into a good-sized tomato ripened to perfection in a field or backyard not far away—a divinely messy way to relish the delectable pearlescent insides and piquant bite of skin while juice dribbles off the chin. For these people, including me, a sandwich made with good bread and a perfect tomato is unbeatable; soft cheese and thick ripe tomato slices (and fresh basil) make a splendid salad; and a refrigerated tomato is a sacrilege.

In spite of spending my early years in the Land of Ten Thousand Lakes—Minnesota—and at the end of the road in Northern Quebec, I was well acquainted with really, really good tomatoes before I came to BC. Tomatoes need sunshine and heat, and these can be found in the long summer days of northern climates. Winnipeg, for instance. My grandmother, a Scottish immigrant thrown into the melting pot that was Manitoba in those days, grew a large garden—including tomatoes—in the backyard to save money while feeding her family. She and her husband came from a long line of thrifty Scots whose odd idea of poverty was growing your own vegetables while a grand piano sat in the parlour.

The result was that in my childhood home, all of us were true tomato lovers, eager to satisfy our cravings every year from late summer until frost threatened. No matter where we lived, we could find our favourites in August: flavourful, juicy beefsteak tomatoes. Sunday mornings found my mom dipping thick slices in beaten eggs, then cracker crumbs before frying them in butter. It doesn't get much better than that.

These days we have expanding, delightful tomato choices: cherry to beefsteak and everything in between, round, pear or oval shaped, heirloom or hybrid, purple, yellow, orange, red or exotically striped. Such bounty.

Cherry tomatoes are actually the new kids on the block. It's hard to imagine salads without them, but they were tough to find before Marks and Spencer in Britain decided to promote them in the late 1970s as a shelf-stable variety. It was a wildly successful campaign. The Greeks and Israelis both now insist they were the first to cultivate the small gems, but in fact, tomatoes the size of peas first grew wild in South America over one thousand years ago. The Mexicans worked to cultivate and crossbreed them to grow larger in size, and in the 1500s, European explorers took the seeds back home with them.

Tomatoes were a tough sell at first in Europe, especially in the north, where they were considered poisonous and used only for table decorations. That doesn't even sound attractive. Pewter plates used by well-off northerners may have been partly to blame, as acid from tomatoes leached out lead, which slowly poisoned the eater. But around the Mediterranean, people adopted the new food with gusto, though it took the Italians until the late 1880s to come up with pizza. The tomato turned out to be a terrific candidate for canning in both sauces and soups (Mr. Campbell's first soup was tomato). Today, over seven thousand types of tomatoes are grown in the field and greenhouses, the second-largest vegetable (well, technically a fruit) crop eaten all over the world.

Tomatoes have been crossbred for uniformity, hard travel and long shelf life to suit the agricultural giants. The difference between in-season, sun-ripened, local tomatoes and those commercially grown far away is impossible to exaggerate. In his book *Tomatoland*, author Barry Estabrook describes fearing for his life as he dodged airborne green missiles flying off an overloaded tomato truck he was following in Florida. He pulled over to examine the errant tomatoes dribbled along the ditch and found they had survived the fall from the truck hurtling along at one hundred kilometres per hour just fine. Green, unripe, perfectly shaped and very hard, they had missed out on their destiny. Tomatoes like them head to warehouses, where they are stored at cool temperatures before being bathed in ethylene gas, a natural ripener, which turns them red (but still very firm) before they head out to supermarkets. This process allows us to buy tomatoes—if you want to call them that—throughout the year.

True tomato lovers want better. BC has a healthy greenhouse business that provides us with pretty tasty tomatoes during part of the winter and spring, but the best way to enjoy truly divine tomatoes is to eat them when they are in season. Most of BC is suitable for

Opposite: It's easy to find an enticing rainbow of tomatoes at farmers' markets—heirlooms and hybrids lovingly grown—all bursting with the flavour of sunshine. Photo: Vince Lee/Unsplash

Cherry tomatoes, now gracing veggie platters and salads everywhere, became an instant hit when they were promoted as a novel variety in the 1970s. Photo: iStock. com/sultancicekgil

growing the crop, but hot spots like the Okanagan produce particularly bountiful harvests. Tomato season starts in July—with the
cherry varieties appearing first—and continues right up until the

first frost arrives, usually in October. Vine-ripened tomatoes do not travel well between the field, the wholesaler and the grocery store, so head to farmers' markets, roadside stands and U-picks to find truly excellent tomatoes. Summer holidays find me searching for roadside stands in places like Lillooet, the scorching sun beating down on my shoulders while I inspect boxes of red beauties to put up into sauces or salsa when I return home.

A rainbow of heirloom tomatoes now graces farmers' markets, a nostalgic nod to yesterday. Varieties like Bonny Best, Tiny Tim and Jaune Flamme have been grown for years, the seeds from the best plants lovingly passed from one generation to the next, each crop producing the same favoured tomato as the one before. Hybrid tomatoes are crossbred, using two different varieties to produce hardy new versions like Green Zebra, Red Robin and Sunrise Bumble Bee, with the best qualities of both parents. Seeds from these types do not reproduce the same tomato, so new seeds must be purchased each season. Luckily, there are no GMO tomatoes on the market, as the Flavr Savr, the first genetically engineered food to be approved for human consumption in the 1990s, went down in flames due to negative public outcry.

When buying tomatoes at the farmers' market, choose a mélange of colours and sizes and take them home to admire in a bowl on your kitchen counter. Never refrigerate. Eat often while the summer wanes. If you end up with a neighbour's unripe green tomatoes, harvested just before frost, place on a windowsill or in a drawer to ripen to red.

To extend the season, slice golden or red cherry tomatoes in half, place cut side up on parchment-covered cookie sheets, brush with olive oil and bake at three hundred degrees Fahrenheit for about one hour. Cool. Now comes the hard part. Try not to pop too many of these sweet-as-candy morsels straight into your mouth as you lay them out on cookie sheets to freeze before tossing into bags. During deep mid-winter, use to top pizzas and frittatas generously for bursts of flavour born in the sunshiny days of summer.

THE THIRST QUENCHERS

Watermelons always bring back memories for me of every August that ever was. Shorter days, cooler nights, school around the corner and backyard picnics before the glory of summertime comes to an end. If I close my eyes, I can picture it. The table, covered in red checkered plastic, is littered with the jetsam of an outdoor meal—chips in bowls, bags of buns, a couple of half-finished salads, squeezable ketchup and mustard bottles and a jar of mayo stabbed with a knife. A man in an apron is at the barbecue, smoke circling around his head. Always, there is watermelon—the vivid pink slices overlapped and arrayed on paper plates between the cutlery and the fluttering napkins. With wild abandon, the kids tear around on the grass in their bare feet, chasing each other, laughing and shrieking. The grown-ups stand, chatting, in twos and threes, feeling lazy and desultory. The sun, having filled the day with heat, is fading a little. Watermelon is dessert for everyone—a thirst-quenching, messy, delicious finish. A sweet goodbye to summer.

Watermelon was born in Africa as a tough, drought-tolerant wild fruit that was prized as a water source by desert tribes five thousand years ago—almost as good as an oasis. Since 2000 BC, these fruits have been cultivated and crossbred to be sweet and juicy. Egyptians loved their watermelons and buried them with their kings—including Tutankhamun—for nourishment and water in the afterlife. Today, the Japanese grow the fruits for the luxury market. On the island of Hokkaido, farmers specialize in raising black Densuke watermelons, which regularly sell for around $200 each. The first of these

Opposite: Because melons need a lengthy dose of heat and sun, they grow best in the hot spots of BC—places like Ashcroft, Lillooet and Osoyoos—that top the temperature charts in midsummer. Photo: Kei Shooting/Shutterstock.com

beauties to be cut from the vine is auctioned off at the start of each season. The record price so far for a single eight-kilogram Densuke watermelon is $6,100, sold in 2008 to the highest bidder.

Japanese connoisseurs have also brought us seedless watermelons using crossbreeding—not GMO tampering—and these have become extremely popular in supermarkets. The small, white, edible, seed-like shells are just empty casings—missing the black seeds that normally grow inside. Naturally, seedless watermelons are sterile—like mules—and growing them is more complicated, which means higher prices. No seed-spitting contests with them either.

The smaller melons, like cantaloupes, are cousins from a different branch of the family. They likely got their start growing wild in Central Asia, then spread east to China and west to Europe, but they were tough to cultivate in chilly northern climates. Pampered King Louis XIV of France kept a greenhouse at Versailles to satisfy his cravings for the fruit. Explorers took seeds to North America, where they were grown with enthusiasm by Native Americans.

All melons love sunshine and heat—the more, the better—and need at least three months of solid summer weather to produce a good harvest. It's tough to meet those requirements in Canada, so the crop is now grown only in the hot, sticky areas close to the border in Ontario, Manitoba and even Saskatchewan, which has its namesake fruit, Cream of Saskatchewan, brought to the province by Russian immigrants. Growing melons near the cool and damp BC coast is an iffy affair, but the hot, dry desert areas in the southern parts of the province are ideal—places like Ashcroft, Lillooet and Osoyoos, which are often declared the hot spots of Canada on summer days.

Today, over one thousand varieties of melons are grown all over the world where the climate allows. The most common types of small melons are the cantaloupe, also called muskmelon, with a rough or "netted" rind and orange insides, and the honeydew, with a cool green rind and interior. These two varieties show up in supermarkets continually and predictably. For most of the year, they are imported from thousands of kilometres away.

In BC, watermelon season runs from August to September, while smaller melons are harvested until October or the first frost. Farmers' markets and roadside stands offer us just-picked BC cantaloupe and honeydew. But growers also try to tempt us with exotic choices they have chosen, like the Sugar Baby or Yellow Doll mini-watermelons, or perhaps the yellow canary honeydew or the Oka cantaloupe, a recently rediscovered Canadian heirloom that is a cross between a Montreal melon—originally grown in a sheltered, warm microclimate area, now swallowed by the city—and a banana melon. Variety is the spice of life, and of melons—both for the farmer and for us.

Five thousand years ago, tough, drought-tolerant watermelon growing wild was prized as a welcome water source by nomadic desert tribes in Africa. Photo: TOONGNA ONLINE/Shutterstock.com

Search for locally grown melons at markets, roadside stands and groceries during August and September—the best are unblemished and heavy for their size. Photo: Brent Hofacker/Shutterstock.com

Locally grown fruits are picked when they are fully ripe, juicy and sweet. Imported specimens are harvested early and unripe—all the better to withstand long-distance travel and increased shelf life, the same as those hard, tasteless Florida tomatoes. Because melons do not ripen after picking, savouring a local fruit harvested at its peak is like relishing a vine-ripened tomato. For taste and variety, it is well worth the effort to buy BC-grown melons at farmers' markets and roadside stands when these succulent summer treats, full of sunshine, appear.

When choosing melons, select those that feel heavy for their size. Avoid any with soft spots, wounds or mouldy stem ends. Watermelons should have a white or pale yellow spot on one side where they sat soaking up the heat and rays in the field. Ripe cantaloupes will smell delightfully of flowers when you have a sniff. Honeydews, however, are sadly odourless. Melons do not need to be refrigerated when whole—a relief when that gigantic watermelon you bought simply won't fit. After cutting, cover with plastic wrap and refrigerate, but devour all melons within days for best taste.

On their own, cantaloupe, honeydew and watermelon are a welcome and refreshing break from heavy, sweet desserts. And all that needs to be done is to slice them or remove the rinds and cut into pieces before arranging attractively on a plate with some toothpicks nearby. The memory of greedily eating one piece of watermelon after another from a buffet, years ago, is seared in my memory. I was pregnant at the time and was seized by a sudden, unquenchable thirst that was slaked only with watermelon. First, I politely took plateful after plateful of nicely cut servings to our assigned table, but I eventually gave that up and shamelessly parked myself right in front of the desserts and finished off all of it. It was, and still is, the best watermelon I have ever tasted.

To move beyond the basics when serving melons, toss together bite-sized pieces of cantaloupe and fresh blueberries—both available, in season, at the same time in BC. Such a lovely colour combination too, especially in a glass dish. Top with a dollop of honey yogurt, or plain yogurt with a drizzle of liquid honey, and serve for breakfast, lunch or dessert.

Watermelon is beautiful on its own but dresses up well. For an impressive debut, cut watermelon in bite-sized squares and thread onto short bamboo skewers or toothpicks, interspersed with fresh mint leaves and slices of feta. Drizzle with a reduced balsamic vinegar, and then sprinkle with some chopped mint and ground pepper. Worthy of a photo before it all disappears.

Ghost Farms

The produce manager and I stood chatting with each other in the damp and chilly backroom of the local grocery store—the realm of the fruit and veggie people. Eau de cardboard assailed my nose and my feet were becoming refrigerated on the cement floor. Surrounded by boxes of bananas and lettuce, the manager talked to me about apples BC apples, to be more specific. His enthusiasm for them was infectious. "Every apple in the store right now is BC grown," he said. I thanked him for that. I wondered how many shoppers noticed the tiny labels stuck on each apple or the signage that told them they were buying local produce in January. How many shoppers knew about the efforts this man was making to carry BC's bounty?

Refrigerated trucks, invented in the 1940s, and countrywide highways, built in the 1950s, changed everything for grocery stores. They made it possible to get fresh (well, sort of fresh) produce from a thousand kilometres away and to have every fruit and vegetable available all year round, as customers have now come to expect— all from just a handful of giant food wholesalers. Fewer salespeople to deal with and not as many cheques to write. Buying from local farmers is far more time-consuming and seasonal. Every produce manager who takes the extra time and effort to sell BC fresh produce is a hero in my book.

Before long-distance transportation became economical, fruits and vegetables had to come from nearby. Farmers all over BC obliged. People had no choice but to eat seasonally most of the time. In our province, we have a litany of ghost towns left behind when mines and mills shut down. In this age of food that travels far from its beginnings, we also have ghost farms.

Norwegians first came to Bella Coola in 1894 to farm because the rugged mountain-ringed valley at the edge of the sea reminded them of their homeland. Photo: imageBROKER/Alamy Stock Photo

A couple of years ago, my husband and I drove to Bella Coola, a place we had never been. We'd been forewarned about The Hill, a precipitous road that winds down from the high Chilcotin Plateau into the Bella Coola Valley, all gravel and nary an abutment in sight. We drove it at twenty kilometres per hour, jaws clenched, as the road steepened and narrowed and the switchbacks became more tortured on the way down. We took furtive glances over the edge into the abyss and tried not to think about driving back up a week later.

At the bottom, it felt as if we had entered another world, cut off from the rest of the province. Driving out toward the sea, the valley widened. Fields appeared, grazed by horses and cattle. Farmhouses out of another time, neatly painted and surrounded by white fences, surprised us. Had we entered another century as well as another place?

Almost. This indescribably beautiful valley, bordered on two sides by high mountains, is a fertile, flat landscape, riven by the Bella Coola River. Streams and creeks run down the steep slopes to join the river on a journey to the sea. Halfway up the BC coast—a jigsaw puzzle of inlets and fjords—Bella Coola lies at the end of North Bentinck Arm and Burke Channel, 140 kilometres from the open ocean. The valley teems with wildlife—salmon, eagles and grizzlies, to name a few. With its mild climate and moderate rainfall, especially where the valley widens away from the ocean, it is perfect for farming too: a secret Shangri-La.

In spite of its isolation, it turns out that food-bearing trucks now make regular trips down The Hill into the Bella Coola Valley. That's why we found Californian and Mexican peppers and tomatoes in a local grocery store that August instead of locally grown. Most of the adorable farmhouses, centred around tiny Hagensborg, fourteen kilometres from the sea, were surrounded by hayfields, not edible crops. We poked around the back roads, finding abandoned farms overtaken by low bushes and spindly alders. Ghost farms. We came across a lonely vegetable stand on the main highway and chose ripe tomatoes, baby zucchinis and juicy cucumbers, and paid by the honour system, stuffing our money into a small wooden box. Many locals have family vegetable gardens, and there are attempts to grow and supply each other with valley-grown food at a weekly farmers' market.

These efforts are being made to regain at least part of what has been lost. At one time, Bella Coola Valley farmers grew apples and pears, cherries and plums, plus a plethora of vegetables, including onions, potatoes, carrots and rutabagas. Some of this harvest travelled by steamship to Ocean Falls, Prince Rupert, Port Hardy and canneries sprinkled among the inlets.

Homesteading began in 1894, when a group of Norwegians were attracted to the Bella Coola Valley. The mountains and the sea reminded them of their homeland, and the BC government struck a deal, offering free farmland if certain requirements were met: clear some land, build a home, barn and fences, and plant crops. Unfortunately, the land claims of the First Nations peoples, who had already been decimated by disease, were barely considered.

The newcomers faced daunting prospects to carve farms out of the wilderness. It required endless back-breaking work, but most settlers persevered to become surprisingly successful at farming by the early 1900s.

Still, it was always a struggle. Constant requests were made to the BC government for roads to get from one farm to another, for substantial wharves and for more frequent steamship service. Recurrent flooding changed the course of the river and washed away fields and even houses. Wild animals destroyed gardens. Weekly steamship service was often delayed because of storms. Within twenty years of arriving, farmers turned to fishing and logging to supplement their meagre incomes.

In the end, there were many reasons that Bella Coola farms turned into hayfields, especially during the second half of the twentieth century. But one of the greatest changes came in 1953, when the residents of Bella Coola built the Freedom Road, a.k.a. The Hill, linking the valley with the Chilcotin Plateau and Williams Lake. Finally, a way out, by road. But access to the outside meant the stage was set for food from far away to invade the valley. Farms have languished.

Salt Spring Island shares a kindred farming history with the Bella Coola Valley. Starting in the mid-1800s, the Canadian and BC governments encouraged immigrants to settle on the island, partly to convince the Americans that this part of the province was not theirs for the taking. British remittance men, with no chance of inheriting land back home, and African-Americans from the United States, hoping for more social justice in Canada, as well as Europeans and even a few Hawaiians, took up the offer for cheap land. Newcomers struggled the same way settlers did far away in the Bella Coola Valley.

In spite of the difficulties, Salt Spring Island eventually became the third-largest tree-fruit producer in the province. By 1894, fruit trees outnumbered island residents ten to one. Salt Spring fruits, root vegetables, butter and meat helped to feed Vancouver and Victoria.

Things began to change for Salt Spring Island when tourism blossomed and people started to buy summer cabins there in the 1950s. Ferry service increased while long-distance food travel flourished. Instead of island-grown fruits, vegetables and livestock being loaded onto steamships to make the crossing to Victoria as they did in the 1930s, trucks loaded with imported food rolled onto ferries at Tsawwassen and Swartz Bay to sail to Salt Spring Island. Local orchards and farms faded away.

My husband and I love Salt Spring Island for its beauty and slow pace. The Saturday farmers' market, a favourite of ours, is always crowded with happy people. It offers a large and luscious selection of locally grown, just-harvested vegetables and fruit. It's hard to choose what to buy because we want to eat it all that night for dinner. Salt Spring Island is coming back to feeding itself, in season. And farmers no longer have to struggle to export their produce as they did in the past; visitors come to them, and specialty foods make their way to the rest of the province. But many farms, like beautiful Ruckle Provincial Park, the site of the once thriving Ruckle farm, are not what they used to be.

Though farming has been lost, it is a comfort to know that the land in the Bella Coola Valley and on Salt Spring Island is still there. We may need it in the future to feed ourselves. But why wait? We can encourage BC farmers all over the province to provide for us the way they did in the past by eating locally grown food whenever possible.

We can buy directly from BC farmers at farmers' markets, roadside stands and U-picks, and order weekly harvest baskets—part of the CSA, or community-supported agriculture program.

But how can we get more BC-grown fruits and vegetables into our supermarkets? These stores are in a position to make the biggest difference in switching to local, seasonal food. The produce managers hold many of the cards. Some of them have more leeway than others when it comes to choosing what they buy, and from where. And all of them want to keep their customers—that's us—loyal and happy. We hold some of the cards too.

What are the best strategies to play those cards well?

Most importantly, know what is in season, month to month, in our province. For example, I know that asparagus in stores during our rainy, snowy January comes from Peru, while in May, during BC asparagus season, it is likely to be local.

When wandering around the produce section, turn into a detective. Check the small print. I look to see if the cherry tomatoes are packed in BC (and grown in Mexico) or hothouse grown right here. I read the tiny labels on the apples. I examine the writing on the sides of boxes loaded with corn. Is it BC or Washington grown?

Learn how to spot the differences between locally grown produce and well-travelled types. I know that dusky, unpolished fall apples and misshapen veggies are likely to be local, and that the delicate colour of a BC peach is unmatched by imports.

Don't be afraid to ask questions. I chat to staff working around me, loading up the lettuce. If California peaches fill the bins in the middle of BC peach season, I ask why. When local harvests are on display, I am outspokenly grateful. The produce people are always touched.

Cast an upward glance to check the signs above each fruit or vegetable. When the origin is not obviously marked, I ask because I want to know what I'm eating. If local produce is not proudly proclaimed with signage, I let someone know. There have been times when I have found BC apples marked as New Zealand. Why would that be? BC-grown food should be celebrated, not ignored.

During our travels last summer, we encountered local corn in a grocery store in the Cowichan Valley on Vancouver Island. There was a handmade poster, written with amateurish enthusiasm and multiple exclamation points, declaring "Local Corn!!!" Miniature BC flags were stuck between the cobs. I wanted to cheer. I took a photo instead. Of course, I bought some for dinner.

FALL

The Time Has Come...to Talk of Cabbages and Kales

Cabbage is a worldly vegetable. It really gets around: Russian borscht, British bubble and squeak, Korean kimchi, German sauerkraut, Ukrainian holubtsi, Japanese okonomiyaki, North American coleslaw, Irish colcannon, Indian cabbage curry, Chinese cabbage stir-fry and New England corned beef and cabbage. So many different ways to enjoy a vegetable.

We've had a long time to figure out what to do with cabbage. Back when we wandered around à la *Flintstones*, wearing skins and brandishing clubs, wild cabbage—a loose-leafed mustard-like plant—grew in northern Asia and around the Mediterranean and up the coast of Europe. It was first cultivated in China thousands of years ago, where farmers experimented to come up with loose-leafed non-heading cabbages like bok choy and tighter, round heading types like sui choy or napa cabbages.

European farmers were thrilled to be able to cultivate cabbage even in their cold northern climes, and by the fourteenth century they had bred hardy, round heading varieties like the smooth reds and greens and the crinkly Savoys. Cabbage earned its keep wherever it grew by producing large harvests on small plots, and it became a major food source everywhere it went.

Opposite: Creative winter cabbage salads, nutritious and tasty, can easily fill in gaps when the only greens available to buy come from thousands of kilometres away. Photo: Alphonsine Sabine/Shutterstock.com

Previous pages: Winter squash, piled high in a wonderful array of shapes, sizes and colours, is a sure reminder that the growing season in BC is drawing to a close. Photo: Adam Cegledi/Shutterstock.com

Cabbages had another attractive quality: many of them stored well. Early-maturing and loose-leafed types, all picked in the summer, didn't qualify. But the dense, heavy, late-maturing soccer balls harvested in the fall could be stored at temperatures just above freezing for up to six months. Through the ages, dishes like cabbage soup staved off starvation for millions while gardens slept during the cold winter months. Cabbage was a genuine hero.

But cabbage had even more to offer. Human ingenuity figured out that lactic acid fermentation in brine made long-term keepers like sauerkraut, with no loss of vitamin C content. Wine-soaked fermented cabbage helped feed the poor souls working on the Great Wall of China. During three years at sea in the 1700s, Captain James Cook proved that cabbage and sauerkraut on board could save sailors from scurvy. All things considered, cabbage was a real crowd-pleaser, for good reason.

It seems particularly unfair that cabbage lost its lustre by the early twentieth century, when it came to be known as a poor people's food in some parts of the Western world. Its reputation suffered further because of the sulphurous odour from overcooking that often went along with it. Happily, things now look brighter for cabbage, as our enthusiasm for vegetables in general and our interest in international dishes have turned us to the cabbage once more. We love our borscht, our kimchi and our coleslaws, as we should.

But try as cabbage might, kale has been hogging the limelight lately. This leafy green seems new to us in North America only because our grandparents didn't eat it. But it was one of the most common vegetables grown and eaten in Europe and Britain for hundreds of years, and has been cultivated even longer than cabbage. Simple to grow and hard to kill—at least in my garden—it was so common in Scotland that people called their gardens kaleyards. Feeling sick was feeling "off your kale." But kale mysteriously disappeared from most grocery shelves on our side of the pond during the twentieth century.

Just like the cat, it came back, available in a slew of choices. Kale is generally divided into three main "tribes." The Mediterranean tribe includes the stunning, dusty-green, bumpy-leafed lacinato. The Scottish types, such as Winterbor, are super curly. And the Russian tribe, brought to Canada in 1885 by traders, includes hardy Siberians, like Russian red, with flatter leaves intersected by pretty pink stems. Farmers' markets offer colours from deep burgundy to blue green, and leaves vary from tightly curled to frilly to lobed—a bonanza of choice.

Other sturdy, slightly bitter greens have come into favour in North America as well, including collards, a close sibling popular in Africa and the southern US; Swiss chard (actually more like a turnip green); and gai lan, also called Chinese kale. It has become a wild and woolly world of greens out there—all the better to discover new and international ways to enjoy what is good for us. Just like cabbage.

For centuries, kale was so common in Scotland that vegetable gardens were called kaleyards, and the expression "off your kale" meant you were feeling sickly. Photo: ivaschishyn/Shutterstock.com

Fall harvests of densely packed red and green cabbage can be stored at just above freezing for months or fermented into sauerkraut so local crops can be enjoyed all winter. Photo: Delaney Zayac, Ice Cap Organics, Pemberton, BC

Cabbage and kale grow all over BC, including in the northern regions. The world's largest cabbage—62.71 kilograms—was actually grown in Alaska. Frost often acts as a sweetener for both. To a locavore, these veggies are winners because they have long seasons.

Early local cabbage varieties—the speedy types like the loose-leafed and miniature varieties—show up in farmers' markets as early as June. These should be refrigerated and eaten fairly quickly. Solid, tightly wrapped latecomers appear in August and September and are sold right out of the field or kept in cold storage to appear in produce sections up until March. These later cabbages store well in the fridge for two weeks or longer.

Kale is hardy and can withstand some frost and even snow. In our warmer areas in the southern part of the province, we can enjoy local kale right through the winter until next year's crop arrives. What could be better? Especially with the plethora of recipes in cookbooks and online for this healthy superfood.

As a local-food fan, I could not make it through winter without cabbage. Borscht features large (see page 189). And coleslaws offer a terrific option to avoid buying those long-distance greens like lettuce. I have a couple of favourites. A mix of red cabbage, celery and green onion, all very thinly sliced, makes a simple, pretty salad, topped with a vinaigrette dressing. Letting this salad marinate for an hour in the fridge makes it even better.

My creamy coleslaw recipe comes from a friend who used to watch her mother make it for her large family back when winter cabbage was a steal. I make it for four or five and it's easy. Put 1½ cups chopped green cabbage and 2 chopped red apples—unpeeled—into a bowl. Add 1 chopped green onion and 3 tablespoons sunflower seeds. For the dressing, whisk together 3 tablespoons each of mayonnaise and milk with ½ teaspoon dried dillweed until smooth. Pour over salad and stir gently to combine. A healthy and tasty take on an old standard.

When it comes to cabbage and kale, we are the world.

GLORIOUS GARLIC

There it was on Craigslist: "Garlic for sale, many varieties, phone Michael," and a contact number. I regularly browse Craigslist, favouring the furniture, farm and garden subcategories in particular, searching for unique treasures. I find them, too. We eat at a Craigslist dining room table while sitting on Craigslist chairs, stack our books on Craigslist side tables and use Craigslist china every day. Each item has a story—a move, a house renovation, an unused wedding gift, a downsizing, an unrealized hobby. Or a harvest of leftover garlic.

Michael's invitation was simply too good to miss, and after work that day I found myself standing in his garage, eyeing box upon box of garlic blanketing several tables—more than I'd ever seen before. The aroma was warm and enticing, making me think of dinner. The local farmers' market had just closed for the season, he said, and these were left from his harvest, unsold.

Young, earnest and dreadlocked, Michael gave me a tour, picking up bulb after bulb, turning them in his hand as he eagerly named and described them. His babies. Russian Red, Leningrad, Persian Star, Siberian, Romanian Red. They brought to mind faraway places and exotic dishes. What kind of garlic silk road had brought them here to this garage? It turns out the fall of the Berlin Wall in 1989 played a role, allowing garlic fans into eastern Europe for the first time in years to collect novel varieties like these and bring them to the West. Michael explained how he came to choose and grow each one—this one for size and shape, that one for bite, and all of them for love. He had to move house and wasn't sure if he was going to

Opposite: Julia Child was a devoted garlic enthusiast, and she played a large role in persuading stodgy North Americans to finally incorporate it into their cooking. Photo: iStock.com/y-studio

be able to grow garlic again. He seemed loath to leave his bounty behind—these cloves, these seeds for next year's planting.

We filled small brown bags with papery-skinned bulbs, pearlescent white and purple striped, large and small, and wrote their names on the outside in faint blue ink because he wanted me to remember them. I spotted a long braid of garlic, and he threw that in for next to nothing. I felt like I'd hit the jackpot. I had my winter supply, plus enough cloves to plant in my garden that weekend. I would have my own homegrown garlic next year.

Garlic has had a checkered reputation since it was first cultivated around five thousand years ago. Originating in Central Asia, it rapidly made its way to the rest of Asia, North Africa and Europe. It is mentioned countless times in the writings of the ancient Egyptians, Greeks and Romans, and right up until modern times, as a medicine. A fitting example of a cure-all, it has been used as a remedy for afflictions ranging from baldness to hemorrhoids, from epilepsy to infections, and everything in between.

Garlic breath, that bugbear, shows up in writings as well, including Shakespeare, who was not a fan. People have long been conflicted about garlic as a food. Pyramid builders and Roman soldiers were encouraged to partake as it was believed to increase strength and stamina, while the upper crust, needing neither of those qualities, disdained it. Much later, the stodgy British were particularly disinclined, looking down their noses at "garlic eaters." During World War II, British spies who went behind enemy lines in France and Spain were given chocolate bars embedded with garlic so they would better fit in with the locals. Medically, garlic juice was called Russian penicillin during the war, as it was used for infected wounds when the real stuff ran short. Pity those poor Russian soldiers.

In North America we were slow to appreciate garlic, in spite of Mediterranean immigrants who showed us the way. When I was a child, any garlic that made it into our house tended to be powdered and in a spice jar, rarely opened and often stale. A delicious exception to our garlicless cuisine was Caesar salad, invented back in 1924, though one famous chef remarked that rubbing the bowl with garlic as instructed was useful only if you ate the bowl. Julia Child, with her enthusiasm for French cooking, helped change our minds. But we were mighty slow learners and it took until the 1970s before most North Americans were using fresh garlic in the kitchen. Now we cannot imagine cooking without it.

There are two types of garlic: soft neck and hard neck. Soft necks have multiple layers of cloves circling around—with annoyingly tiny ones near the centre—and soft stems that can be braided. China has overwhelmed the garlic market, growing 80 percent of the world crop, all soft-neck varieties that can be mechanically planted and harvested. Chinese garlic shows up everywhere in our grocery stores.

BC farmers grow mostly hard necks, which have a single layer of large bulbs around a stiff stem. They suit our climate but demand more attention. Each clove must be planted by hand, point up, roots down, in October. The roots grow down into the soil all winter, even under snow, preparing the plant to send up green shoots of narrow leaves in March. By May they attempt to procreate like all growing things, extending up to form garlic scapes, which curl over elegantly like swans, with unopened flowers close to the delicate pointed ends. These scapes, now popular in the kitchen, are snipped off by hand to send extra energy into bulb formation under the ground. In August, after the green leaves start to die off and turn yellow, the garlic is harvested by pulling the bulbs out of the dirt. Next, they are cured by storing in an airy, dry spot for two weeks so the bulbs harden enough to last through the winter.

It is easy to buy several months' supply of BC garlic in late summer and fall at farmers' markets and groceries that specialize in locally grown food. The best bulbs are hard and bulge slightly with cloves. Never refrigerate, as when the garlic is taken out, it will sprout. Instead, keep it at room temperature and never bag it. Set out these beguiling bulbs as part of your kitchen decor.

While soft neck garlic can be braided into plaits to artfully decorate the kitchen, most farmers in BC grow popular hard necks with evenly sized cloves. Photo: Nicola Valentine

I use garlic almost every day and it has a starring role in my hummus. It couldn't be simpler and it's healthy enough to devour shamelessly without guilt. Rinse one 540-millilitre can of garbanzo beans (chickpeas), add water to cover in saucepan and set on the stove to simmer for 5 minutes. Let drain for at least 30 minutes and then put into a food processor with 1 crushed clove of garlic, 1 tablespoon olive oil and the juice of 1½ lemons. Process till smooth, adding more lemon juice if necessary to get the consistency of a dip. Serve with crackers and cut-up vegetables—carrots, celery and cherry tomatoes are best. Glorious garlic—what would we do without it?

PEARS: GIFTS OF THE GODS

In my family, we had a tradition of finding secret, abandoned places. We'd jump in the car and my dad would take us down twisting, narrow back roads, the dust rising in our wake like a ribbon. Peering out the open windows, we'd search among the trees for evidence of the past. Unusual clearings in the forest or signs of habitation, hinted at by weather-beaten logs or boards, all merited investigation. My dad would stop the car and we'd tromp through the bushes and tall grass to explore. One of our favourite spots, which we returned to year after year, was an old farm set in the back hills of Minnesota, long ago deserted. Crabapple trees dotted the overgrown field, and snitching one of the tiny fruits to bite into—a mouth-puckering explosion of taste—seemed forbidden, sort of sneaky. But there was never anyone there, no one to see.

As a grown-up, I found my own hidden places. When my husband and I moved into a brand-new bungalow on a typical suburban street, not far from the centre of White Rock, I unexpectedly came across one. At the end of the block, there was a path leading into a messy deciduous forest, begging to be followed. One fall day, I wandered in among the cottonwoods, the afternoon sun flashing brightly, flickering through the leaves and branches. There they were: pear trees, just off King George Highway near the US border. Their limbs reached skyward, twisted and gnarled, showing the ravages of time. I wondered what sort of farm I was trampling on, left behind long ago. There were pears, dangling low among the green, tempting me. They were hardly model fruits, looking as if they too had suffered a hard life, blemished with brown. Most were too high for me to reach, disappearing into the greenery above me, but I picked as many as I could, stuffing them into my pockets, cradling them in my cupped hands.

Pears are picked when they are "mature," not ripe. Unlike most tree fruits, pears ripen to perfection off the tree—most often in our kitchens after we buy them.
Photo: Dan Gold/Unsplash

As I walked home, I thought of pies and fresh eating, but it was not to be. Every tender pear I cut open was brown and mushy inside, ruined and overripe. I was too late.

It turns out that most pears are among the only fruits that must ripen off the tree. They are picked when they are "mature," not ripe—like unopened cut flowers that bloom later in a vase. If allowed to remain too long on the tree, pears begin to ripen from the inside out so that by the time the outside feels just right, the inside is overripe, like the secret stash I picked.

We've had eons to get pears right. As far back as the Stone Age, they grew wild in the Caucasus Mountains, which divide Europe from Asia. From there, they spread in both directions to give the world European pears to the west and Asian pears to the east. It is simple to cross-fertilize pears and experiment with unique seedlings, so what started as a few wild types expanded, with human tinkering, to over three thousand varieties available today.

Asian pears went their own way and now look almost like apples. Also called Chinese, nashi or apple pears, they are grown all over Asia as a popular fruit. They are crisper than European varieties, with tender, bruisable skins, and can be eaten right off the tree.

European types developed quite differently in shape and texture. In days gone by, most were too tough for fresh eating and needed to be cooked. Early chefs braised, baked, poached and fermented the fruit in dishes like pear patina, a cooked egg and mashed pear dish favoured by the Romans, who brought the fruit to western Europe. By the nineteenth century, Belgian fruit breeders were fiddling and fussing to eventually produce pears with lovely buttery insides—called beurre pears—similar to those we eat fresh today.

Pear trees are hardy souls and can be grown all over BC, even as far north as Prince George. Most commercial varieties—almost all European types—are grown in the more favourable soils and climate of the Okanagan, Similkameen and Kootenay Valleys. Bartlett, D'Anjou and Bosc are the most common, but smaller growers and homeowners can experiment with a myriad of exotic choices.

European pears are picked when they are just barely changing colours but still hard. Most harvests are stored just above freezing for a time before landing in farmers' markets and grocery stores. This cold treatment is required before ripening can properly take place. When brought to room temperature, pears soften over several days to transform into the fruit we love, with smooth juicy insides and tender skin. Putting them in paper bags (especially along with a banana) can hurry the process along by bathing them in ethylene gas, a natural ripener given off by fruits. Pears can pass from prime to overripe in what seems a moment, so they need watching. How to tell when they are ready for eating? The flesh should give a little when you press down lightly with your thumb near the stem, which should be easy to pull out. Who knew achieving pear perfection was so complicated?

When buying European pears, choose hard fruits without dents or bruising. Superficial marks are fine—and give the pear a little

character. Who wants a boring pear? Bartletts mature by mid-August, and we can be eating them by the end of the month. Bosc and D'Anjou pears are harvested a month later. Fortunately for us, they can be kept cold for months, like apples, to keep us supplied over the winter—Boscs until January and D'Anjous right up until March. If you've scored a large bag, take out only as many as you want to eat in the next couple of weeks and keep them at room temperature. Stand back and admire how they look—especially those long-necked, dusky Bosc beauties. Stick the rest in the fridge for ripening later. If you end up with too many ripe pears, refrigerate them to stop further softening.

One of the best things about pears is that they can be inventively included in a meal from start to finish, in appetizers, salads, entrées and desserts. And that doesn't even include eating them fresh. What adaptability! It hardly seems fair that they play second fiddle to more popular apples.

When I have enough ripe pears, I love to bake them into pies and crumbles—sometimes along with very thin apple slices or a sprinkling of blueberries, though they are divine all on their own. If I have only one or two, my favourite way of enjoying their wonderful subtle flavour is in a salad. I slice them, unpeeled, arrange them attractively on a bed of greens and drizzle my favourite reduced strawberry balsamic vinegar back and forth across the pears. I top with whole roasted pecans—baked for ten minutes at 350 degrees Fahrenheit and cooled—and serve right away. The ancient Greeks called pears the gift of the gods. When savouring a salad of juicy fresh pears in the middle of winter, that sounds about right.

Opposite: During the nineteenth century, Belgian fruit breeders fiddled and fussed to finally produce pears with lovely buttery insides—called beurre pears—similar to those we eat fresh today. Photo: Robyn Mackenzie/Shutterstock.com

TALES OF TERROIR

Who doesn't love the word *terroir*? A glorious word, difficult to pronounce and slippery to define. It has a tendency, at least for non-francophones, to roll around inside the mouth, seemingly forever stuck in there. The *Larousse* one-word definition is "soil," but we know it is much more than that. A combination of land and tradition, terroir is the idea that taste is affected not only by where, but also by how food is grown, and by whom.

We have borrowed from or, more correctly, shared this word with the French, who commonly use it to distinguish between different sorts of cheeses and wines. But why not use this charming word that connects us to the earth and farmer to describe other foods? Carrots, for instance. And rutabagas.

The Pemberton Valley, north of Whistler, is flat and long, hemmed in by stunning, impossibly high peaks running down both sides. Farms radiate out from the centre, horses graze and summer heat shimmers, trapped between the mountains. Independent organic growers are snapping up more and more small acreages to intensively grow, then sell, fresh produce at markets and to the restaurant trade.

But the original farm business of the valley was growing seed potatoes, many distributed to our neighbours to the south. Chances are those Idaho potatoes in the produce aisle—which are actually just russets grown in Idaho—were born as Pemberton seed potatoes. But farming families like the Hellevangs and the Beks, longtime seed potato producers, also grow carrots in the sandy soils of their land far up the Pemberton Valley. Locals call this area the Meadows. The sun, the rain, the soil, the climate and the farmers

Opposite: Purchase rutabagas in the early fall as they will be sweeter than the tough warehoused baseballs that eventually make an appearance in March. Photo: iStock.com/kershawj

together grow unmatched carrots—in what turns out to be the perfect terroir. Sweet, juicy and bright orange, these Pemberton carrots turn anyone who tastes them into hopeless and irrevocable carrot snobs. I should know; I am one of them.

Carrots are roots, and to be the best they can be, they have to head straight down into soft dirt as they grow. If they hit a rock on the way, off they go in different directions. Rock beats carrot. The sandy loam of the Pemberton Valley is an ideal soil recipe for root vegetables. Over thousands of years, volcanic ash from an eruption of Mount Meager at the valley's north end and glacial melt created a flat flood plain with few rocks. Regular flooding, now mitigated by dikes, further enriched the soil. For a carrot, it doesn't get much better than this.

The Hellevangs and Beks are picky about what kind of carrots they grow. Among the hundreds of available varieties, they choose a Nantes type, known for its juicy sweetness. Unlike the long, tough and pointy grocery store versions, these carrots are stubby with rounded ends. Being a tender breed, they are unable to withstand harsh mechanical machine digging and must be harvested by hand. The carrots are also chosen with weather in mind. Because they mature later in the fall, the carrots can be left in the ground until, ideally, they are kissed by frost. The chilling converts some of the carrots' starch into sugar, making them even sweeter and more impossible to resist.

It turns out that the terroir of the Pemberton Valley is perfect for another root vegetable as well: rutabagas. The mere mention of this humble food makes normally broad-minded people grimace while claiming they never touch them. The unlovely name alone seems reason enough to skip these pale yellow, purple-topped globes in the supermarket. Even the produce guys rarely let the word *rutabaga* fall from their lips, choosing to refer to them quietly as turnips, even

Opposite: Purple and yellow carrots seem exotic and new but actually were grown for hundreds of years before the novel orange upstarts showed up in the 1600s. Photo: iStock.com/Wildroze

though they know better. (There is confusion, but turnips are different: smaller, most commonly white with purple tops and harvested earlier in the season.)

I admit I came late to rutabagas. It was not until I tasted the beauties grown in Pemberton by the Hellevangs that I became a fan. Divinely sweet and tasting nothing like what most people imagine, this locally grown vegetable now routinely makes its way into my stews and soups.

BC-grown rutabagas and late-maturing carrots show up in earnest at markets and stores before Thanksgiving. While Pemberton carrots may be hard to find, aim for a similar sweet taste by looking for shorter, stubbier Nantes carrots. Purple and yellow varieties are

available, but surprisingly, they are neither new nor exotic, having been grown for hundreds of years before the orange upstarts (cross-bred in the 1600s) made a splash. Orange is the new purple—who would have thought? Nantes carrots tend to disappear from markets by Christmas, being less likely to survive long, cold storage than their pointier relatives, so catch them while you can.

Look for local newly harvested rutabagas at this time of year too, as they will be sweeter than the tough warehoused baseballs that eventually make an appearance in March. Buy several in the fall and store them in the back of the fridge. For a dependable, simple side dish, steam a peeled, diced rutabaga along with two to three peeled, diced potatoes until fork tender (Cut the rutabaga into smaller pieces than the potato.) Add one-half cup plain yogurt and smash together with one of those wavy potato mashers. Lumps are okay. Serve hot, immediately. Don't tell anyone what's in it until all second helpings have been devoured.

As the days darken, it's time to put foreign leafy greens aside and create winter salads with hardier, local ingredients. Root vegetables make a welcome diversion from cabbage coleslaws. Grate half a peeled raw rutabaga and two carrots. Add a few snipped green onions and try the following Asian dressing, which complements the vegetables: two teaspoons each of lemon juice, rice vinegar and honey, one teaspoon soy sauce and one tablespoon sesame oil, whisked together.

At one time, rutabagas were good for more than the table. Up until a generation ago in Ireland, Scotland and Britain, they were carved into ghoulish faces and lit with candles to frighten off evil spirits on All Hallows' Eve. The tradition was brought to North America, where pumpkins, bred on this side of the pond, took over the starring role at Halloween. Bring the rutabaga back and carve a gargoyle face into the surface and scrape a hollow at the top for a candle. A novel centrepiece to toast the locally grown fall bounty before the land sleeps and the farmers rest.

TOUGH SISTERS

We know the growing season is drawing to a close in BC when a parade of winter squash appears in grocery stores and farmers' markets. The fluted acorns, the smooth creamy butternuts, the dark green kabochas, the ghostly blue Hubbards and the aptly named two-tone delicatas. They look like they belong in a still-life oil painting rather than in the kitchen. With them comes the smell of fall, a nip in the air, the portent of change.

They arrive just when we need them, after we've said *sayonara* to the summer squashes we've recently enjoyed—little pattypans, funny crooknecks and mountains of zucchini. All squashes are seeded into the ground in late spring, but summer varieties are harvested earlier when still immature, with small, tender seeds and soft skins. Winter squashes grow for up to two more months, and as adults they have tough skins, hard insides and mature, roastable seeds. They show up in plenty of time for Thanksgiving dinner. We use one of our most beloved winter squashes—the pumpkin—to celebrate the fall season with jack-o'-lanterns and pumpkin pie.

But winter squashes come with a bonus: they can be stored, sometimes for months. The "winter" in winter squash actually refers to when they are eaten, not when they are harvested. Luckily for us, that means that we can eat local butternut squash, for instance, in January.

Storing winter squash is not without its issues. Most squash has to be properly cured, sitting somewhere warmish and airy for a couple of weeks after autumn harvesting to slow respiration (yes, these veggies breathe) and to develop thicker skins and extra sweetness. Usually the farmer performs this task, sometimes right in the field, to supply us with winter squashes ready for keeping. When buying, choose specimens with short stems (except for stemless acorns) and blemish-free skin that cannot be pierced with a thumbnail. Never use stems as handles; cradle squash in your arms like something precious.

In this age of giant refrigerators, we tend to think everything lasts longest when chilled. Not so. Winter squashes like it guest-bedroom or basement cool: ten to fifteen degrees Celsius. Maybe even by the front door—fall decor with a plus. When cured and stored the way they should be, acorns and delicatas last for four weeks and kabochas do well for three months, while Hubbards and butternuts can plod on for six months. Ideal for winter eating.

A couple of years back, I thought I had all this well in hand and artfully arranged a pleasing variety of sizes and colours of winter squash along the top of my old upright piano in my chilly family room. Then I forgot about them. By the time I remembered to check on them—cued by a slight odour and thinking of soup for supper—one of the pumpkins had melted into liquid, running down the inside of the piano, where some of it remains to this day. A cardinal rule of vegetable storage: check them once in a while, or just buy them at the market in January and let the farmer or wholesaler do the storing for you.

Like many people, I find winter squash a tad intimidating, as cutting them up while keeping all ten fingers intact can seem challenging. Splitting a large Hubbard, for example, can involve a big, big knife, a mallet, an axe or dropping it from a height onto a hard floor. Barbara Kingsolver, in her book *Animal, Vegetable, Miracle: A Year of Food Life*, hilariously relates how her mother looked on askance as she and her surgeon father—who was surely at ease with sharp instruments—took turns attacking a sizable pumpkin with a monstrous knife.

As with most things, knowledge, advice and experience in squash dissection are invaluable. Novices can start with softer, smaller

Opposite: For centuries, the "Three Sisters"—squash, beans and corn—provided a healthy diet when grown by Indigenous Peoples in North, Central and South America. Photo: MNStudio/Shutterstock.com

squash like the delicata. With any winter squash, often the best way to begin is to cut off the ends and/or slice in half to get flat surfaces for stability on a cutting board. To soften the skin first, squash can be microwaved on high for two to four minutes (turn over halfway) or baked at four hundred degrees Fahrenheit for twenty minutes. Scraping out the seeds and stringy bits comes next. Halves can then be baked to provide soft innards for pie or muffins. Halves can also be sliced for oven roasting with a glaze or spices—try brushing with maple syrup and a sprinkle of cinnamon. They can also be peeled with a potato peeler (or a knife after slicing) and cut into squares to

simmer in soups or stews. Who doesn't love a heartwarming soup of cut-up squash simmered in broth with favourite spices, then puréed? As one of our most versatile foods—used in both sweet and savoury dishes—winter squash is simply too good to miss.

Humans have been squash eaters for around ten thousand years. First appearing in Central and South America, squash, along with maize (corn) and beans, formed one of the Three Sisters that were so important to indigenous diets in the Americas. The early European explorers, while not particularly impressed with the vegetable, carried the seeds home. It took until the 1800s for Europeans to embrace the food with gusto—especially around the Mediterranean, where Italians and French still revere their own special varieties, such as heirlooms like Marina di Chioggia and Galeux d'Eysines. Africa, India and Asia are thought to be earlier adopters, possibly because squash from the Americas conveniently floated over to their doorsteps.

Winter squash grows anyplace summer sunshine and heat abound. In BC, that can be anywhere, but the Okanagan, the Lower Mainland and Vancouver Island are particularly blessed. Because cross-pollination—either by man or nature—is common, there are hundreds of winter squash varieties in a myriad of colours, patterns, sizes and shapes, with smooth or warty skin. Look for unusual and heirloom types from around the world at fall farmers' markets. To appreciate the diversity in the squash world, head out to size up the biggest at a local fall pumpkin contest. At the world-recognized competition at Krause Berry Farms in Langley, winners top out at around 540 kilograms. The best way to cut up one of these giants? A chainsaw. Try *that* in your kitchen.

Opposite: Look for unusual winter squash varieties in a myriad of shapes, sizes and colours in the fall—perfect for savoury, hearty soups or sweet baking. Photo: Taylor Kiser/Unsplash

CRANBERRY CRAVINGS

My family makes jokes about my fondness for cranberry sauce, which, I admit, is somewhat extreme. At holiday turkey feasts, they humour me and place a dish of the stuff on the table next to where I sit—a little pot of crimson delight just for me. Even then, sometimes I need a refill. I simply cannot do turkey dinner without it. Only once has this happened—and that was enough.

I was a guest. The table was set for twenty-four and it looked impressive—water glasses, cloth napkins and lots of sterling silver lined up on dark polished wood. Filling a spacious dining room— tailor built for it—the table was a lengthy affair that had come, along with the hosts, from some English manor many years before. About once a year, we gathered for a sumptuous meal at the invitation of these friends of my in-laws. The lady of the house—a delightful woman with sparkly eyes and a cap of curly blond hair—was experienced at entertaining and handled predinner socialization and food prep like a pro. Menus varied, but trifle, the pièce de résistance, invariably finished things off. Everyone always enjoyed these evenings, including the cook herself.

One of these dinners featured a traditional turkey feast. The birds were carved, the gravy made, the potatoes whipped and the stuffing ready. We served ourselves from giant platters, but as we moved toward the table, I noticed something was missing. There was no cranberry sauce. How could that be?

Perhaps it had been forgotten. I asked—and the host, with a puzzled look, said they never ate it. Much to my chagrin, that didn't

Opposite: Native cranberries were grown around the Hudson's Bay post at Fort Langley in the early 1800s and were more valuable for trade than salmon. Photo: Sergei Drozd/Shutterstock.com

stop her from searching through one cupboard after another, looking for something that would serve the purpose. Finally, she handed me a jar of strawberry jam. I meekly took it to the table.

Now, anyone who is familiar with cranberries knows that they are at the tart end of the berry spectrum and strawberries are at the other, sweet end. The jam jar remained unopened. My turkey was fine, topped with heaps of gravy, but it could have been tastier. Nowadays, I always come bearing a gift for turkey-dinner hosts: my homemade cranberry sauce.

Cranberries, like turkeys, are native to North America, and the two were likely eaten together long before the Pilgrims celebrated

the first American Thanksgiving in 1621. The berries grew in wet bogs and marshes in temperate climates around the continent. Indigenous peoples picked them for food (raw, cooked or dried), for medicine and for dying cloth.

Cranberries flourished in the southern and coastal areas of BC as well. After a Hudson's Bay trading post was established at Fort Langley in 1827, cranberries became important for local trade. The boggy land around the post was perfect for the wild berries, and First Nations people picked them to trade for blankets. At one time, these little reds were more valuable than salmon, as they provided a hit of vitamin C when added to the dismal diets of sailors to prevent scurvy. The cranberries were packed and shipped from Fort Langley to San Francisco in hundred-pound barrels, a measurement still used for today's harvests.

The first cranberries were not cultivated until 1816 in Massachusetts, meaning they are relative newcomers to farming. Two hundred years is a mere blip in the history of agriculture. A fussy plant, cranberries cannot be grown just anywhere. They require a watery soil made of peat, clay, sand and compost. In BC, most are grown in the Fraser Valley with a smattering on Vancouver Island.

The cranberry is a short plant—a ground cover, really. Runners grow close to the earth and send up shoots, which bear flowers that, when fertilized by bees, produce berries. Slow off the mark, the bushes take five to six years to produce a good crop. That's a long time to wait if you're a farmer who must prepare a field with ditches and irrigation to keep the berries happy in a damp environment. But it pays off for generations—of humans that is—as bushes plug away for sixty to one hundred years or more.

British Columbia produces the third-largest crop of cranberries in North America. Harvest time runs from September to November, when the berries have turned a burnished crimson. Most fields are flooded with water—knee deep—the night before picking. Machines, nicknamed egg beaters, splash around to detach the berries, which float because each one has four little hollow compartments inside (cut one in half to check). The floaters are then collected to send off to process into juice or sauce, or to be dried. Only 10 percent of the entire crop goes for fresh or frozen whole berries, and these are dry harvested by machines that comb berries out of the bushes with giant metal teeth. No swimming for them.

When buying fresh berries, look for hard shiny rubies in the fall. When perfectly ripe, they will bounce when dropped onto the floor. Fresh cranberries can be tossed into the freezer in bags or containers and kept for nine months. Usually, fresh and frozen berries are interchangeable for any recipe.

I like to sprinkle a handful of the little jewels into my apple pies— they add a burst of flavour and look pretty too. I add them to muffins and breads, often with a dash of orange juice or zest. But my favourite way to use cranberries is in cranberry sauce. I start with one 340-gram bag of berries, fresh or frozen. I put them in a pot with one-half cup of water and set it on to boil. When things start to bubble, I turn it down to a simmer to thicken. Berries will eventually burst with the heat, but gently pressing with a potato masher speeds things up. When all are softened, and a few whole berries remain, I add one-quarter cup of sugar to sweeten, heating to dissolve. The result is a gorgeous, tart sauce unmatched by any canned or jarred versions. Being the hopeless fan I am, I confess to never making one batch—I make two at a time. Sauce can be made well ahead of the great turkey event—even the day before—and can be served cold or lukewarm. Either is heaven.

Putting Food By

Every year in July, my husband and I pick raspberries. It is always hot and buggy. We wear long sleeves, pants and baseball caps sprayed copiously with insect repellent. The sun blazes as sweat runs down our foreheads and drips onto the ground from our eyelashes and noses. We mash our way into the tall raspberry bushes at North Arm Farm in Pemberton, reaching out for beauties hidden among the thorns, leaves and cobwebs. We listen to the singsong voices of children in the next row, Mom doing the real picking while the kids throw unripe berries, branches and bugs into their pails. Mustering on, we fill ice cream bucket after bucket. Our goal is to freeze enough to last us through a winter of raspberry-topped ice cream and yogurt smoothies.

Our efforts in the berry patch make us feel good in a knowing-where-your-food-comes-from kind of way. But our work also makes us part of a tradition as old as humanity: we are "putting food by." Before the age of well-travelled food, late summer and fall saw families hoarding the harvest like squirrels. Winters were long, and people still had to eat while gardens slept.

It was serious work keeping hunger at bay when most food was local. Kitchens were warrens of activity in the late summer heat while knives chopped and pots burbled. Heaps of tomatoes were canned, cukes pickled, fruit dried and cabbage fermented. Apples were picked, potatoes and carrots dug out of the ground, and onions and squashes laid out to cure in the weak autumn sun—all to be stashed in root cellars to keep through the winter.

Being a locavore in winter is tough. The produce section, looking ample as always, doesn't make it easy either. Eating local requires thinking like a pioneer and understanding how harvests, fresh from the ground, are kept. It means finding local food that has been frozen, canned or chilled in cold storage.

Freezing food, like our raspberries, is a simple way to store the local harvest. In *Little House in the Big Woods*, Laura Ingalls Wilder describes how Pa hangs frozen bear meat in the back shed during winter, to be cut off in pieces with an axe and cooked by Ma. Long before Laura, the Inuit stored meat in permafrost dugouts. By the 1940s, newfangled fridges with freezers made it possible to keep frozen food all year in every climate.

In a perfect locavore world, it would be easy to find locally grown foods in grocery store freezers. But BC frozen-food packers often have to gather harvests from far away to ensure an adequate

In 1858, tinsmith John Mason invented sealable lids for his glass jars, which meant people could can foods at home in their own kitchens. Photo: Zigzag Mountain Art/ Shutterstock.com

supply. There are exceptions. Most frozen blueberries and cranber-ries packed in BC are local because we grow prodigious amounts of them. Cast your eye over the fields in Richmond or Ladner. All those stick-like bushes grow berries. Some farms and markets sell their own frozen berries at harvest time. If you are stuck with a tiny fridge-top freezer in rental digs, look for frozen berries sold all year long with a "BC grown" label. Rhubarb, too. And maybe if we all jump up and down in the frozen food aisle, insisting we want more BC-grown frozen foods like corn and peas, we'll get them too.

A favourite film of mine, *Meet Me in St. Louis,* opens with a scene in a large old-fashioned kitchen. It's 1903, and the housekeeper stands over the wood stove, stirring a steaming pot of homemade ketchup. The women of the family drift in and out, tasting and med-dling: it needs more sugar, or vinegar, or spice. Of course it's Au-gust, when tomatoes ripen. I love that scene.

Today, it's different. We don't have housekeepers (wouldn't it be lovely?). Maybe we don't have room for all those jars (tiny con-dos) or a way to haul a bushel of fresh tomatoes home (use a wagon instead of the bus?) or even a desire to make all that ketchup. But every time we snag a can of tomatoes or garbanzos off the grocery shelves, we are using the relatively recent innovation of canning to keep food.

Sadly, it was war that spurred the invention of canning. Napo-leon coined the phrase "An army marches on its stomach." He wasn't kidding. In 1795, he offered a 12,000-franc reward to anyone who could devise a way to safely preserve food so his armies could feast on something other than beer, wine, salted meat and whatever they could pillage. Frenchman Nicolas Appert had been fiddling around for years with sealing food in containers and finally won the contest in 1810. The large canisters (now called cans) had to be individually soldered, often with lead, filled, sealed and then boiled for hours, but it worked. There was another problem: soldiers had to bayonet or bash the cans against rocks to get inside, as the can opener was not invented until forty years later. Talk about slow learners.

In 1858, the tinsmith John Mason patented a new sealable lid for his glass containers, called (surprise!) Mason jars, and brought canning into our kitchens. By the twentieth century, with leaps and bounds of innovation and an understanding of micro-organisms and botulism, canned food was available and affordable to everyone.

Today, we can at home by choice, not necessity. We are able to enjoy home-canned delicacies, labour-free, by happily scouring farmers' markets throughout the winter. Jewel-toned jams, pickles, chutneys and fruits beckon, all lovingly prepared from local summer bounty.

As a child, I was enchanted with my grandmother's dim and mysterious basement, cool even in a hot Prairie summer. Intriguing items from my beloved grandma's past surrounded dusty shelves filled with preserves of questionable vintage. Though not an official root cellar, her basement served the same purpose. Root cellars, traditionally built underground or dug into a hill, kept food cool while protecting it from freezing. They were used to store root vegetables and fruits, onions, winter squash, canned food and even homebrew.

We can easily follow this tradition and eat locally without digging up our backyards. Around the province, locally grown veggies like potatoes, parsnips, rutabagas, carrots and beets, and fruits such as apples and pears, are perfectly kept for months at temperatures just above freezing in cold storage. These foods magically appear in markets and produce sections all winter long. In the supermarket, I check my choices carefully. I search for labels that tell me the food is grown in BC and ask about provenance if necessary. Local potatoes win my heart over US spuds every time. Ditto for Okanagan apples and pears over New Zealand world travellers. I'm picky. After all, I have high standards: my frozen Pemberton raspberries are second to none.

WINTER

BEHOLD THE BRUSSELS SPROUT

Like most young children, I thought my father knew everything there is to know. So when he told me that Brussels sprouts were the best vegetable in the world, I believed him. At least, for a while. Conservative in his eating habits, he insisted this green vegetable— one of the few he would eat—join the turkey, dressing, mashed potatoes and cranberry sauce on our plates every Christmas. Since he hailed from Scottish stock, his preference was not unusual: the British eat more sprouts than any European country, especially on December 25. Eventually, I learned his enthusiasm was not shared by everyone. In the United States, Brussels sprouts hold the dubious honour of being the most hated vegetable in the country. Pity the little green cabbages.

I actually like Brussels sprouts. Perhaps familiarity bred affection, or warm memories of festive meals—or my father—influenced my taste. Every year, I look forward to these miniatures coming into season at the same time as holiday decorations. A bright green vegetable, grown right here in BC, available fresh in darkest December—how wonderful is that?

After leaving my childhood home, my affection for Brussels sprouts endured. Ensconced in Vancouver suburbia, I discovered a roadside stand that satisfied my search for the freshest sprouts and set me on the path to becoming a locavore. The Eng Farm in Surrey offered vegetables picked that very morning in the field behind the

Opposite: A most peculiar-looking vegetable, Brussels sprouts usually take four months to produce up to one hundred sprouts budding off sturdy, leafy stalks. Photo: Anastasiia Malinich/Shutterstock.com

Previous pages: Photo: freestocks.org/Unsplash

stand, and twenty dollars scored a box filled to overflowing with fresh bounty. I was hooked. The season started with lettuces, green onions and radishes and ended with root vegetables, winter squash and Brussels sprouts.

I discovered that these little cabbages so loved by my father did not grow all ready to cook like in the supermarket. The Engs sold them still attached to the stalk, marching like little round soldiers—buds, actually—around and up the sides of a sturdy stem. I had never seen Brussels sprout plants growing in the field, so these multi-packs—so long they barely fit in the box—were a complete surprise to me. At home I could cut them off as desired to cook for dinner. I was utterly charmed.

Like most plants we eat, the origins of Brussels sprouts are fuzzy. It turns out they are not little cabbages at all, though they

It is likely that Brussels sprouts were named after the capital city of Belgium, though no one seems to know why. From there, they spread northward, where they were embraced with gusto. Photo: Keenan Loo/Unsplash

are cousins in the brassica family. Cruciferous vegetables, or brassicas, likely started out in the wild as mustard-like plants growing around the Mediterranean. Farmers cultivated and crossbred them, working their magic over hundreds of years to come up with wildly varied results, including Brussels sprouts, cauliflower, broccoli, kale, kohlrabi and cabbage, to name a few. It seems probable that sprouts were named after the city of Brussels, as they showed up in Belgium during the Middle Ages before making the rounds to the rest of Northern Europe and the UK, where they were embraced with gusto.

In the field, Brussels sprouts like it cool—preferring a temperate climate—so they can be grown all over BC. They are the tortoises of the vegetable world, taking three to four months or longer to grow from seed into stalks 60–120 centimetres high, each with an impressive 75–100 sprouts budding between large, sturdy leaves. Full grown, they are one of the most peculiar-looking crops to be found in a farmer's field—think miniature Amazon jungle. Harvesting generally runs between October and December. A light frost sweetens the crop, and they can be picked even while frozen, which explains why my grandmother sent my father out to the backyard to dig them out of the snow in Winnipeg.

It is best to eat the local harvest fresh—not frozen—from the field, a treat to be savoured long after most green veggies have signed off for the season. And, whether you are a five-fruits-and-vegetables-a-day adherent, a sort-of vegetarian or a strict vegan, these miniatures pack a punch. Along with fibre and antioxidants, a serving of Brussels sprouts has more vitamin C than an orange. My father was wiser than I thought.

When buying, pick sprouts that are bright green (unless reddish varieties are on offer), with tight, firm heads and white bases. It's worth choosing sprouts that are about the same size so they cook equally, and, as usual, smaller is better—sweeter and more tender. Refrigerate right away, and expect them to last up to a couple of weeks.

Brussels sprouts have truly come into their own in the kitchen. No more boiling them until soggy and squishy so they release an unpleasant sulphurous odour—which brings to mind nineteenth-century novels set in tenements with eau de cabbage in the hallways. Now we enjoy our Brussels lightly steamed, oven roasted, stir-fried or chopped raw in salads. So many delightful and delicious choices.

I realized early on that the microwave is a perfect way to steam Brussels. Select sprouts of the same size, trim the bottoms and remove loose outer leaves. Microwave, covered, on high with a little water until just barely tender. Serve with butter. Fast and odour-free, this is a cooking method best reserved for true fans, like my father.

More creativity is required to entice those who make unattractive faces at the mere mention of the vegetable. Many recipes involve bacon—which almost seems like cheating. Instead, try stir-frying sprouts with Indian spices to make a tasty side dish. Prepare similar-sized sprouts and slice in half to make about one and a half cups. (This recipe can also be made with a combo of cauliflower pieces and Brussels sprout halves.) In a frying pan with a tablespoon of olive oil, toast one teaspoon each of mustard seeds and grated fresh ginger with one minced garlic clove on medium high for five minutes. Those who like heat can also add their favourite hot spices here. Add Brussels sprouts and stir-fry, browning them, then add small amounts of water and cover to steam lightly. Sprouts are done when they can barely be pierced by a fork. Do not overcook! Remove from heat and sprinkle with lemon juice. Serve warm. Be prepared for compliments. Bow and behold the Brussels sprout.

THE THIRD INGREDIENT

In 1908, the beloved short story author O. Henry—famous for his tale of self-sacrifice "The Gift of the Magi"—wrote a gem entitled "The Third Ingredient." It features two hungry, down-on-their-luck young women who meet in a boarding house over the making of a stew. One has the meat; the other, the potatoes. There are persistent, pointed laments about the lack of an onion, as in: "A stew without an onion is worse'n a matinee without candy." After all, how can anyone make a tasty stew without onions?

Indeed. Onions are the unsung heroes of the vegetable world. Almost always a bridesmaid and never a bride—French onion soup being an exception—they rarely get their due. Yet the first words in a recipe are often "Sauté chopped onion until soft." And who hasn't had their appetite whetted, their mouth water, at the scent of onions frying in the pan?

Julia Child weighed in with "It's hard to imagine civilization without onions." She was spot-on. According to the UN, they are eaten and grown in more countries than any other vegetable. Ninety percent of harvests are eaten within the country in which they are grown. That would make onions both the most global and the most local vegetable of all.

Onions, like all vegetables, started out in the wild—where they still grow. But these savoury orbs were one of the first plants to be cultivated—six to seven thousand years ago in or around Central Asia. And onions figured large in the world's oldest known cookbooks, written for Babylonian chefs on clay tablets. When cuneiform script was finally deciphered in 1985—four thousand years after being inscribed—recipes like deer stew and fowl pie, with onions, leeks and shallots, came to light.

Today, we are as keen on the edible alliums—members of the onion family—as the Babylonians were. All of them, including garlic, can be grown in BC. The first ones to make a seasonal appearance are green onions, a welcome sight in early spring. Like most alliums, these can be grown from "sets"—small bulbs—or from seeds. They are ready to harvest when the green shoots grow tall enough to cut or pull and before underground bulbs have a chance to form.

Despite being classified as an herb rather than a vegetable, chives are bona fide members of the allium family as well. Milder and finer than green onions, they also appear early in the spring. If left to their own devices—that is, if not cut down at the knees to harvest—they produce showy puffball flowers pretty enough for cutting.

The allium oldsters—shallots and onions—take more time and thrive in the heat and sun of BC's dry areas, so long as they get regular drinks. The bulbs, hiding underground, slowly grow larger beneath green shoots. Regular onions produce one bulb each, while shallots grow several smaller bulbs in a cluster, like garlic. They are both ready for harvesting when the green tops start to dry out and fall over. After pulling, onions need to cure for a week or two—sitting on top of the soil in dry sunny weather or laid out under cover—developing crackly outer skins and firm insides so they can be stored.

Leeks are the tough guys in the family. Seeds or baby plants are planted in troughs, which are gradually filled in with soil as they slowly grow, ensuring the bottoms remain a tender and subterranean white. Able to withstand frosts, they are one of the few vegetables that can be harvested—pulled out of the ground—all winter in BC's most temperate climates: the Fraser Valley and Vancouver Island. In other words, a locavore's dream.

But BC-grown regular onions, cured to store well for months, are a perfect addition to the pantry in wintertime. Last fall, when my husband and I squeezed in a late-season camping jaunt to Kamloops, hitting a farm stand on the way home was part of the plan. In particular, I was on the search for onions—a big bag to last through a winter of soups, stews and sauces.

We found what we were looking for near Cache Creek—set smack in BC's desert landscape of dried grass and sagebrush. The stand was loaded: plums, pears, peaches and nectarines; peppers in an array of yellow, red, purple and green; field and plum tomatoes, all in bulk and by the case. Out back, piles of cabbages, a jumble of Brussels sprouts still attached to their stems, and heaps of winter squash—butternut, kabocha, acorn and spaghetti—filled wooden bins. An overwhelming horn of plenty. Two women, oddly overdressed in high

Opposite: After they are pulled from the soil, onions need to cure by basking in the sun or under cover for a week or two so they develop crispy skins and hard insides for storage. Photo: rootstock/Shutterstock.com

"It's hard to imagine civilization without onions," said Julia Child, quite correctly. Onions are grown and eaten in more countries than any other vegetable. Photo: Barbro Bergfeldt/Shutterstock.com

heels and lacy black outfits, wandered in and drifted among the bounty. They peered, they poked, they squeezed and then, somewhere in the vicinity of the Brussels sprouts, one of them couldn't seem to help herself and cried out, "This is just like Christmas!" Exactly what I was thinking. Making off like bandits, my husband and I gleefully stuffed boxes and bags of fruits and vegetables in among the camping gear, including a twenty-five-pound bag of beautiful golden onions.

If you missed out on the farm stand, never mind. Look for local leeks and onions at winter farm markets and in the produce section. Some onions, like Walla Walla, Spanish, Vidalia or red onions, are mild enough to be used raw or cooked, but will not store as long as stronger-tasting white and yellow onions. BC-grown is best, but dry, hot eastern Washington is known for its onions, and they beat California-grown types in travelling time.

When buying, search for hard, unblemished onions with crispy skins. Store in a dry place at room temperature, preferably in a mesh bag or laid out in a single layer. Van Gogh loved to paint onions. Get the same look by arranging them on a pretty plate on the counter—a perfect way to store them. Keep them away from other fruits and veggies to avoid mingling flavours and moisture. Once cut, keep in the fridge.

And now, back to O. Henry's story. Those two hungry, onionless young women eventually encounter—most improbably—a young man roaming the boarding house halls, holding in his hands…wait for it…one giant onion. Naturally, they all share, they all eat, two fall in love and it's happily ever after.

Onions, leeks and shallots are featured in the oldest cookbooks in the world, written for Babylonian chefs on clay tablets thousands of years ago. Photo: Lisovskaya Natalia/Shutterstock.com

For your own stew story, you'll need: 3 cups beef broth (water plus bouillon cubes will do in a pinch); about 450 grams beef stew meat; 3–4 carrots, sliced; 3–4 potatoes, cut into large chunks; and 2–3 onions, quartered. To start, brown the meat in a little olive oil in a large pot. Pour in just enough beef broth to almost cover the meat, and then add 2 tablespoons each of brown sugar, cider vinegar and ketchup, plus 1 teaspoon Worcestershire sauce, a bay leaf and 1 smashed garlic clove. Simmer for 1 hour, stirring occasionally and adding more broth as needed. After the hour is up, add the rest of the broth, carrots, potatoes and onions. Bring to a boil, then reduce and simmer for another hour, or until potatoes and carrots can easily be pierced with a fork. Combine 2 tablespoons cornstarch and ½ cup cold water, stir until milky and smooth and add to stew. Bring to a boil and burble until gravy is thick and translucent—not long. Put on the fire, dig in and savour the essential third ingredient.

A Root and a Tuber Met
in a Bar...

When I was working to cover my university fees, books and fun money, I ended up with a one-night gig at a legendary nightspot just across the border in Washington State. Not even old enough to walk past the bar (let alone partake) at the time, my sister and I were hired on as extra kitchen help for an anticipated overflow crowd. Hamburgers, hot dogs and fries were on the menu—food we could whip up in our sleep with our past experience as short-order cooks. But this establishment featured something new.

Instead of using the usual precut frozen fries, the spuds were freshly prepared right there. Filling an entire corner was an enormous machine that looked more like an instrument of torture from the Middle Ages than something that belonged in a kitchen. The metal bowl-shaped contraption, huge and battered, reached almost to the ceiling and rotated relentlessly, like a cement mixer. Large, washed russet potatoes were loaded in the top, and the monster, grinding away with a throaty sound, literally rubbed the skins off with its rough interior. The potatoes eventually found their way to the very bottom, where they were squeezed out through blades, emerging magically as raw french fries. We were fascinated. The evening was spent dropping baskets of these spuds into deep fryers to serve hundreds of patrons "home fries." Needless to say, there were some pretty big bags of potatoes lying around.

Opposite: Pemberton, north of Whistler, is called Spud Valley for good reason: it supplies seed potatoes to farmers in Canada and the western United States to grow next year's crop. Photo: Nikolay Antonov/Shutterstock.com

It turns out that *pommes frites* (french fries) really did originate in France in the late eighteenth century, where they were served in fashionable restaurants. It took almost two hundred years, but they eventually became a howling success the world over, from fish and chips to McDonald's. But we all know there are better, healthier and classier ways to eat potatoes.

Potatoes have played a major role in human history. First cultivated on the cool slopes of the Andes, potatoes were selected and bred from a variety of wild plants that grew all over South America.

Since beets can be stored for many months, we can enjoy them cooked or grated raw in salads, soups, side dishes and even desserts all year round. Photo: Sarah Stewart, Rootdown Organic Farm, Pemberton, BC

Early European explorers took them to Europe in the 1500s, where they were viewed with suspicion. People found the spooky eyes and rough bumpy skin slightly creepy. Poisonous, evil and disease caus- ing, they figured. In truth, the leaves of both the potato and toma- to (another initially maligned food) are toxic to humans. War and famine changed everyone's minds. When Europe experienced grain crop failures, or fought wars on farmland, people turned to pota- toes to feed themselves.

The Industrial Revolution was fed by potatoes too. Because it was easy and quick to grow a large harvest on a small parcel of land, fewer people were needed on the farm, and that allowed workers to head into cities to find jobs. Populations boomed as families were better fed because of the plentiful, nutritious vegetable. Ireland alone grew from five million to over eight million people between 1800 and 1845.

It is ironic that a vegetable that saved people from starvation in Europe caused the Irish Potato Famine. In an early example of monoculture at its worst, poor Irish tenant farmers relied heavily on a single variety of potato to feed themselves—breakfast, lunch and dinner. But in 1845, a fungus blight began to spread from Europe to Ireland, and when it arrived, it rapidly killed the only crop that kept 30 percent of the population fed. One million died of starvation, and over a million left the island. Not only have we changed the plants we eat, but they have changed us.

Blight is still a problem today but resistant varieties are available, and potatoes still feed much of the world, including potato-loving eastern Europe and Russia. Developing countries are growing more than ever. But while the potato is becoming a hero in parts of the world, its fortunes are declining in most developed countries, where preferred diets do not necessarily include them. A pity.

Potatoes can be grown easily in most places in BC, though the largest harvests come from the Lower Mainland, Vancouver Island and the Okanagan and Kootenay Valleys. In spring, pieces of last year's spuds—called seed potatoes—each with two or three eyes, are buried in the earth. These send out gnarly subterranean white shoots and send up leafy green plants to soak up the sun. Some of the underground stems, called tubers, swell into potatoes—usually between three and ten for each plant, depending on potato size. Digging for them is like finding hidden treasure. The season starts in June for small early potatoes and carries on into October for larger spuds. Late varieties are harvested for both fresh eating and long-term storage to keep us in potatoes until next year's crop arrives. That means we can eat BC-grown spuds all year round.

I could not live without potatoes. I buy my winter supply directly from farmers since I live close to Pemberton, also known as Spud Valley. My favourites are reds and yellows. I bake, I scallop, I mash. I love the creamy texture of these potatoes baked in their jackets. Russian purples—as intensely coloured inside as out—early nuggets and sweet, smooth fingerling spuds round out my choices.

When buying potatoes, look for hard, blemish-free specimens. Before cooking, cut away any greenish parts, caused by toxic solanine, which is produced in old potatoes or those exposed to light. Choose same-size spuds for easy baking. To speed things up, I start bakers, washed and poked with a fork several times, in the microwave. I turn them over halfway, cook until fork tender and then finish in the oven at 350 or 400 degrees Fahrenheit for twenty to thirty minutes to make skins crispy.

Unlike potatoes, beets are rising stars in North America with an enhanced nutritional status. Completely unrelated to spuds, beets were cultivated from wild chard-like plants that grew on the coasts of Europe and around the Mediterranean. For hundreds of years, only the leafy above-ground parts were eaten, while the swollen red roots were used as a cure-all medicine. Europeans, especially the eastern potato lovers, eventually realized that the deep crimson roots made for excellent eating as well. Think borscht. Australians love their beets too—Aussie burgers are often served with a slice of pickled beet instead of the standard dill. And beets are the new health food for many.

Beets are grown from seed, starting in spring. Leafy tops hide red roots underneath the ground. Farmers' markets now offer Chioggia beets, striped like candy canes inside, and golden varieties too. Small, young beets show up in June with their leafy tops attached. When buying, look for fresh-looking, crisp greens and hard beets. At home, trim tops off and store separately from the roots in the fridge to avoid beet dehydration. Late-summer beets are larger and are sold minus their leafy tops. Like potatoes, these store well for months, so we can buy BC-grown beets in markets and grocery stores for much of the year.

Today, we enjoy our beets pickled, cooked or grated raw in salads, soups, side dishes and even desserts, providing a marvellous, intense shot of colour. Fresh beet greens can be treated like spinach—barely cooked or used fresh in salads.

Cooking beetroots requires patience. I give them a good scrub, leaving the root on the bottom and short stems on the top, then put them in a pot of water to boil and turn down to a simmer. Then I wait. And wait. I poke them with a fork now and again to test for tenderness, and about an hour later, they are done. After cooling, skins slip off easily. They are perfect to slice on a plate and top with feta, toasted pecans and a few snips of something green—Italian parsley or arugula will do. Finish with a vinaigrette.

My favourite recipe for beets (with potato of course) is borscht. Cut 5 or 6 small-to-medium-sized cooked beets into small pieces and add to a pot with 3–4 cups chicken or vegetable broth (bouillon cubes in water will do in a pinch). Add 1 medium chopped onion, 1 smashed garlic clove and a 398-millilitre can of chopped tomatoes (with liquid). Next, add the rest of the veggies: ⅓ of a medium-sized green cabbage, thinly sliced and chopped; 1 good-sized carrot, grated; and 1 peeled potato, chopped into small pieces. Lastly, add 1 teaspoon each of dried dillweed and sugar and ¼ cup white wine vinegar. Bring to a boil and then turn down to simmer for an hour. Top with sour cream when serving. A rich, hearty fall soup that can't be beet.

LONG PAST HARVEST

One February long ago, my husband and I headed up to Big White for a few days' diversion. On our way back to our motel late one afternoon, après après and still clad in ski duds, we stopped for dinner at a marvellous little Italian restaurant in old downtown Kelowna. We satisfied our hunger with a fine pasta feast, woozy with post-skiing fatigue and cocooned in candlelight on a gentle snowy night. For dessert, our server suggested—wait for it—an apple. So we sliced and munched our way through two of the largest, juiciest, crispest, sweetest-tasting apples we have ever had. The word *locavore* was not yet invented in those days, and we innocently asked the server where these delectables came from, thinking far, far away. He stepped back, shocked and dismayed. (Truthfully, it was more like disgust.) "Here, of course!" he declared. That's when we found out just how long an Okanagan apple can last when it's stored the way it should be.

Most BC apples, like those we savoured that mid-winter evening, are grown on the sunny slopes of the Okanagan Valley. Orchards are also cultivated on Vancouver Island and in the Similkameen, the Kootenays and the Fraser Valley. Farmers grow apples organically and conventionally, including Gala, Red and Golden Delicious and Granny Smith, plus our very own made-in-BC varieties like Spartan (a 1926 original), Nicola, Aurora Golden Gala and Salish, a recent addition. No GMO fiddling was involved in birthing these apples—just old-fashioned cross-pollination, grafting or serendipity.

Sometimes, nature transcends all. Apples are the rebels of the fruit world, and when grown from seed, they do not grow "true"— meaning they refuse to take after either of their parents. Each and every seed unpredictably reinvents itself, just like a teenager. It is genetic diversity run amok, which has earned the scientific mouthful "extreme heterozygosity." A chance sprout from an unruly seed took root in Sally and Wilfrid Mennell's Similkameen orchard in 1991, looking different than any they had seen before. They propagated it because of its tasty fruit and named it Ambrosia, a BC favourite.

Such lucky finds are rare, but they have happened before. Red Delicious, Golden Delicious and McIntosh apples all began as random seedlings. One day in 1868, sixty-nine-year-old Maria Ann

BC born and bred, Spartan (a 1926 original), Nicola, Salish and Ambrosia (sprung from a rogue seedling) apples flourish on the slopes of the Okanagan Valley. Photo: Marina Khrapova/Unsplash

Fresh new crops of BC apples appear, crisp and milky, every fall as winter looms, but when stored just above freezing, we can enjoy them right through spring. Apple crisp anyone? Photo: AS Food studio/Shutterstock.com

Smith, an orchardist, tossed the core of an apple she'd eaten onto the ground outside her home near Sydney, Australia. The result of her untidy habits was a rogue upstart bearing a tart green apple, which she decided to propagate and sell as her own special variety. She did not live to see her apples become one of the most popular in the world: Granny Smiths.

The world of apples presents a dilemma. How do farmers grow the kinds of apples they want over and over if they can't use seeds? To get a true copy, they must take branch cuttings or buds from the tree they want to multiply and attach—the official word is "graft"— these to other apple tree trunks to grow into a new plant. Generation after generation, favourite apple varieties are propagated in this time-honoured way. Does this mean that more than one kind of apple can be grafted and grown on the same tree? Yes, it does.

A few years ago, my husband and I spent an idyllic week in Northern Italy in South Tyrol. We biked and hiked around a gorgeous, mountain-ringed valley filled with apple crops. There was not a single tall and graceful tree in sight. Rows and rows of short, espaliered plants, growing flat against wire fences, covered the gentle slopes. More productive and easier to tend and pick, this is the way many apple trees are now grown in BC as well.

Usually harvested between August and October, apples fill grocery and market bins every autumn, newly plucked, with a natural milky coating, smelling like fall and oh so fresh. Biting into the tart, mouth-watering, juicy crispness evokes the taste of waning, chilly days, watery sunshine and the promise of winter.

Unlike soft fruits (like cherries), apples can be stored. After picking, they continue to breathe and ripen, which makes them shrivel and wrinkle after a few days at room temperature. If kept just above freezing, however, ripening is put on hold, and they can last for months. Apples from BC are stored this way in cold-storage facilities and shipped out to grocery wholesalers and markets throughout the winter. That means we can buy BC apples in our local stores right up until June. How good is that?

All fall and winter we have an embarrassment of riches to choose from—an array of apples, heaped in red, green and yellow mounds, looking like baubles. Washington and BC apples sit beside incredibly well-travelled specimens from New Zealand, Chile and South Africa.

So, what to pick? As a locavore, it's no contest. Washington apples are better than any that have crossed an ocean, but BC apples trump them all if we want to eat locally and continue to have apple orchards grace the slopes of the Okanagan Valley. How to tell a BC apple from a foreign job? Look for posted signs or small stickers on the apples that say they were grown here. If the apples' provenance remains a mystery, ask the produce manager. Someone, somewhere in the back among the damp banana boxes and discarded lettuce leaves, knows the answer. With a little care, we can still get the taste of Okanagan sunshine in mid-winter.

Purchased apples need to go into the fridge, pronto. When placed in a lovely arrangement on the counter they quickly lose crispness and flavour. In spite of our best intentions, we can all end up with a few shrivelled and abandoned apples rolling around the crisper drawer—for shame! But that's why apple crisp, a heart-warming winter dessert, was invented.

First set the oven to 375 degrees Fahrenheit. Then combine the crumble part in a bowl: ½ cup each of brown sugar, flour and rolled oats, ¾ teaspoon cinnamon and nutmeg, and finally ⅓ cup melted or soft butter. Use your fingers or a fork to mix. Peel, core and slice about 4 medium-to-large-sized apples directly into a well-greased 20-by-20-centimetre (8-by-8-inch) pan. The apple slices should create a layer about 4 centimetres thick on the bottom of the pan. Sprinkle the crumble topping over the apples and pop in the oven. Bake until the apples are soft, about 30 minutes. (Poke a fork into the crisp to be sure.) Serve warm, with ice cream or whipped cream if you have it. Make this satisfying dessert to celebrate Apple Month in BC—February—a timely reminder that apples are available for our eating pleasure long past harvest.

FUNKY FUNGI

We were fungi eaters long before Alice bit into a mushroom on a caterpillar's advice. In the fantastical world of Wonderland, her first nibble made Alice shrink alarmingly, and her second sent her up to dizzying heights. That about sums up our relationship with mushrooms—in a word, crazy. Dangerous and delectable, intoxicating and inexplicable, mythical and medicinal. Since prehistoric times humans have looked at these wonders with two minds: mycophiles, those who love them; and mycophobes, those who fear them.

Fungi have been around for millions of years. They are neither plant nor animal, but a strange separate living being. They do not require sunlight and do not use photosynthesis to make their energy, but feed on the dead and decaying below them. Fungi actually share more DNA with animals than with plants. Endless mycelia—small root-like threads—spread under the ground like a mat. When it's time to reproduce, as all living things must do, fungi send mushrooms above ground like periscopes—sexual, spore-producing oddities that can appear in mere hours. A single spore, held in the underside gills, can start new mycelia.

The sudden appearance of something where there was nothing was a puzzler and the source of many a myth. In the British Isles, mushrooms emerging overnight—sometimes called fairy rings—were thought to be leftover umbrellas from nighttime fairy revelry or, alternatively, the devil's work. Europeans called them witches' or sorcerers' rings. Stepping inside the rings was thought to bring doom, luck or fertility; take your pick. By the Victorian era, mushrooms experienced a pleasant redo. Called toadstools, they regularly appeared in fairy tales as cute furniture for elves and pixies. One variety—red with white spots, oddly patterned after a

In the 1800s, brown button mushrooms were cultivated in the catacombs under Paris on horse manure—an enterprise that was halted when the Métro was built. Photo: iStock.com/g215

toxic, hallucinogenic sort—graced children's books and front yards as lawn ornaments, as they still do today.

The early Romans and Egyptians were way ahead of the superstitious British and Europeans, and ate mushrooms with relish and reservations. Wealthy Romans called them the "food of the gods," hired experts to search the woodlands for them and used dogs or slaves as testers, just to be sure. Commoners were excluded. The Chinese called mushrooms the "elixir of life" and knew their fungi well enough to start cultivating them around the seventh century.

King Louis XIV of France was a fan in the 1600s, and, happily for him, it was discovered that mushrooms could be cultivated on horse manure in the catacombs under Paris. Chefs embraced them with such enthusiasm that they were called Parisian—actually button—

mushrooms. By 1880, there were three hundred mushroom farms under Paris, but the Metro eventually halted the enterprise.

Truffles, the "diamonds of the kitchen," became a popular delicacy by the late 1700s. Harvests were sniffed out by specially trained dogs or pigs in Provence and Northern Italy. The description is apt: truffles are still one of the most expensive foods in the world.

In BC, experienced pickers gather mushrooms in the damp, dimming days every fall. The best spots are jealously guarded. Harvests are inspected and purchased at roadside stands to be sold to restaurants and wholesalers, and to be exported to Japan.

I have had the pleasure of hiking over spongy moss, a peaceful pastime, searching for treasures alongside a mushroom expert. However, with slim pickings and a lack of knowledge, I left the woods behind. I now head to the grocery store to buy cultivated mushrooms—a recommended course for anyone but the experts.

Cultivation of mushrooms around the world is now common. China is the top world producer by far, though not all mushroom cultivation is large scale. In Vietnam, while touring the wetlands outside Hue, we encountered large heaps of straw piled up into beehive shapes, kept specifically for growing mushrooms for a family. Small Canadian farmers grow shiitake mushrooms on logs for the specialty market. In France, independent champignonnières grow Parisian button mushrooms inside old quarries.

In BC, commercial mushroom cultivation is a carefully controlled process beginning with compost. Farmers either buy or make their own, starting with animal waste (usually chicken manure), straw and recyclable gypsum. After decomposing nicely, this mixture is pasteurized by raising the temperature for seven days. The finished compost—known as substrate—is seeded with "spawn," which is mushroom talk for seed-like starters. The seeded substrate is then covered with a layer of peat moss, the barns made cozy and toasty, and the magic begins. Within about fourteen days, tiny mushrooms pop up, and seven days later, the full-grown crop covers the peat moss like a blanket. Picking takes place over three to five days, and then everything is left to rest for one week before the next cycle, or "flush," of mushrooms appears. Harvesting is done two more times. The substrate is pasteurized again to kill all mould and bacteria and is then removed to be used as a soil conditioner, added to potting soil or used to grow earthworms. The mushroom farmer starts all over again with new compost. Rotating multiple crops ensures the mushrooms never stop.

The most popular cultivated mushrooms are the white button variety, followed by cremini or brown mushrooms, then portobellos, which are just overgrown creminis. Shiitake, oyster and enoki varieties are grown by specialty mushroom farmers for a small but growing market.

When buying mushrooms, I prefer to pick and peck at loose specimens, finding the sizes I want. But whatever you choose, mushrooms should be damp (not slimy), firm and smooth with unwrinkled tops, and uniformly coloured. I find brown mushrooms are firmer and tastier. Refrigerate right away. Though opinions differ, I generally keep mine in a paper bag.

People wonder how to clean mushrooms. Those brown bits cause consternation, even though growers ensure us that these are just pieces of peat moss and perfectly harmless. My mother-in-law used to peel mushrooms completely. No wonder she didn't buy them often. Even farmers differ in their advice: some say rinse under a cold tap (like I do); some say wipe with a damp cloth or mushroom brush. Whatever way you choose, clean them just before using and slicing.

Today it's easy to enjoy mushrooms in countless ways, like on pizza. We make ours from scratch and it just isn't the same without the fungi. To avoid any sogginess, we microwave sliced mushrooms for a minute or two first, pour off the juice, then decorate the pizza.

Stuffed mushrooms make a wonderful appetizer, perfect for potlucks. To make, start with 12 medium (4-centimetre) brown mushrooms. First, clean the mushrooms any way you like and trim off dirty ends. Using a knife as encouragement, twist out all the

Though wild mushrooms grow only in the fall, the cultivated variety is different. BC mushroom growers rotate their crops to provide us with year-round harvests. Photo: zi3000/Shutterstock.com

stems and set aside. Finely chop 1½ tablespoons each of kalamata olives and sun-dried tomatoes (squeeze out oil first) along with the mushroom stems. Sauté everything in a frying pan with 1 teaspoon olive oil for 2–3 minutes—just until mushrooms are cooked and any liquid has evaporated. Cool slightly and add 1½ tablespoons of feta crumbled into tiny bits. Sprinkle with dried or fresh basil and mix together. Fill mushrooms, pressing down slightly. Place them in a 20-by-20-centimetre (8-by-8-inch) pan and cook at 350 degrees Fahrenheit for 20–25 minutes. There will be juice in the pan, so you will want to move the mushrooms to a plate to serve. These are hearty, filling starters, so 2 per person should suffice, though there will be enthusiastic fans. Just make sure you get your share.

Under Glass

Let's not fool ourselves. Even committed locavores get a little tired of cabbage and carrots in wintertime. Thankfully, just when we really need them, tomatoes show up in March—juicy, sweet and BC grown. We can thank our own greenhouse growers for these welcome edibles.

Driving out to the Tsawwassen ferry terminal, it's hard to miss the giant glasshouses spread over the farmland to the left of the highway in Delta. They are just the tip of the iceberg. There are now over sixty greenhouse farmers in our province, growing cucumbers, peppers, lettuce and tomatoes. Most are in the balmy Lower Mainland, with a few on Vancouver Island and in the Okanagan and Kootenay Valleys. It is such a successful enterprise that BC ships large quantities of hothouse vegetables across the border.

Greenhouses, or hothouses, are not new. There was a flurry of enthusiasm for them in seventeenth-century Europe to coddle the new and exotic plants explorers found in distant, warmer lands. Many ships had botanists on board, and when they returned with their treasures—no thoughts of invasive plants back then—they wanted to grow and study them, often for medicinal use. As well, it became all the rage for the wealthy to build personal glasshouses to grow pineapples and oranges, just because they could. But it was difficult to heat and ventilate them properly. By the mid-1800s the Victorians and the Dutch managed to make improvements. It didn't hurt that glass became cheaper and more plentiful at the same time. Cities like New York, Vienna, Paris and London tried to outdo

Opposite: Greenhouse tomatoes, close and cozy, are trained to climb up supports. With no frosts to kill them and a long growing season, they grow several metres high. Photo: The Motion Arts/Shutterstock.com

each other by building enormous glass buildings, filled with tropi-
cal plants. These crystal palaces were open to the public, allowing
urbanites to commune with nature by strolling among the orchids.

Today, growing vegetables (and flowers) in greenhouses is big
business. The Dutch are on the top of the hothouse heap, and others
take their cues from them. These are fine-tuned operations, involving complicated computerized heating, ventilation and watering
systems. Most are hydroponic—meaning soilless—and grow plants
in coco fibre (from coconuts), rockwool (from basalt and chalk) or
sawdust. No dirt means no weeds—so no herbicides. Organic certification includes soil and compost management, so without any dirt,
greenhouse vegetables cannot be declared organic. (There is at this
writing, however, one hothouse farmer in BC who grows in soil and
has obtained the certification.)

The inside of a greenhouse is a well-ordered jungle. Tomatoes,
cucumbers and peppers are trained to climb along strings and make
their way to the upper reaches of the hothouse. Plants can reach
up to twelve metres in length—not surprising as these veggies are
oldsters—living for up to eleven months with no frosts to kill them.
Plants are close and cozy in long rows, their water and nutritional
needs perfectly addressed. These ideal conditions pay off big time;
greenhouses can produce as much as ten times the amount that can
be grown in the same area outside in the field.

Water requirements for greenhouse vegetables are lower than
for those grown outdoors due to less evaporation. Rainwater is collected to irrigate the plants at most greenhouses, and water, mixed
with nutrients, is recycled again and again so there is little or no
waste. Whenever possible, carbon dioxide produced from heating is
circulated back into the greenhouses for the plants to use during photosynthesis. Some hothouses use shades to prevent heat loss at night.

Greenhouses are a closed shop. To avoid contamination by in-
truders—from viruses to bugs—outside visitors of the human sort
are not encouraged. Whenever possible, integrated pest management is used to deal with insect infestations. Hungry ladybugs and

The inside of a greenhouse is a well-ordered jungle, and under ideal conditions plants can produce up to ten times more bounty than out in the field. Photo: DutchScenery/Shutterstock.com

tiny wasps are released to eat pesky aphids and whiteflies. These predators have company; tomato blossoms are fertilized by resident bumblebees, which buzz around and live a sheltered life.

Despite growing in an unchanging, cloistered environment, hothouse tomatoes, peppers and cucumbers do have a season in BC. By the third week of November, growers shut down, remove plants and give the greenhouses a good scrub at a time when daylight is short and temperatures are low. Sometime in December large seedlings—mostly hothouse-raised in BC with artificial lights—are planted. With natural daylight, it takes until March for tomatoes, cucumbers and peppers to be ready for harvest. The growing season continues up until November. The gap in supply—November through March or so—is filled with veggies imported from other greenhouses down south in places like California and Mexico. Most hothouse vegetables are appealingly packaged to catch our attention. The only way to tell if they are locally grown is to read the fine print. Watch for "BC grown" or "Product of Canada" labels.

All greenhouse-grown vegetables are hand-picked when ripe. Tomatoes are vine ripened, unlike others that grace our stores in winter—those long-distance travellers that are picked green and ripened with ethylene gas. Local greenhouse growers (call them indoor farmers) offer a myriad of choices. Hothouse-grown BC tomatoes come in sizes and shapes from petite grape tomatoes to plum to beefsteak. Peppers are available in yellow, orange and red, small or large, and bell or pointy. Long English cucumbers are joined by petite versions. Lettuce, mostly of the butter sort, is grown all year round. Because they are raised in controlled environments, hothouse veggies tend to be perfectly shaped and coloured—almost surreal. Farmers continue to experiment, searching for new crops, and eggplant has now joined the crowd.

Though nothing will replace peppers, tomatoes and cucumbers grown in season, outdoors, for me, I welcome these wintertime treats to ease the wait until summer arrives. An excellent way to enjoy all three together is a time-honoured Greek salad. For a slightly different take, it's easy to make an Israeli or Middle Eastern salad. Cut equal quantities of cucumbers (no need to peel), tomatoes and peppers into small pieces the size of peas. Add finely chopped onion if you like. Toss with a vinaigrette made of lemon juice and olive oil in equal amounts, briskly stirred. The fresh and juicy taste of this salad in March is a delicious and colourful reminder of the bounty soon to come. Savour with gratitude and anticipation.

WALKING THE LOCAVORE WALK

Canada is known as the Great White North for good reason. But compared with the rest of the country, those of us who call British Columbia home have it easy. Most of us live in parts that are downright balmy. The Lower Mainland and Vancouver Island are rated the best growing zone in Canada, and our entire coastal climate, right up to Haida Gwaii, is milder than anywhere else in the country. We are doubly blessed because we have multiple fertile, flat river valleys tucked between our mountain ranges, like the Fraser, Okanagan, Pemberton, Kootenay and Bella Coola Valleys. And our northern latitudes bring extra hours of sunshine to help make up for short summers. Even though only 5 percent of our total land area is arable, BC farming packs a big punch and offers us a cornucopia of locally grown food.

How can we benefit from our good fortune and take advantage of the local fruits and vegetables that hard-working BC farmers grow to feed us? It turns out that we have a healthy assortment of options to help us find and enjoy the bounty. Even trying one or two strategies can make a difference. Here's the list:

KNOW WHAT'S IN SEASON

This is the big one. We need to know what BC farmers are growing and when they harvest their crops. When produce sections look the same all year round, it's easy to lose track of the fact that all edible plants have a season.

Spring, summer and fall are when plants and farmers in our province work overtime. In the marvellous, diverse world of BC-grown fruits and vegetables, some emerge early in spring, like asparagus, greens and strawberries. Others prefer the heat and sun of

Community-supported agriculture (CSA) weekly harvest boxes are a sure way to get the freshest and best a local farmer has to offer during the entire growing season. Photo: stockcreations/Shutterstock.com

summer, like tomatoes, cucumbers and peaches. Some take their time and ripen in the fall, like apples, winter squash, cabbages, onions and the subterraneans, such as potatoes, rutabagas and carrots.

And all plants need a rest—a time to go to seed and sleep before springing to life once again. In BC, that's winter, when rain, snow and chill rule. There is no way to cheat this plant life cycle, except with greenhouses.

Luckily for us, those late bloomers, like apples, potatoes and cabbages, store well for months and keep us in fresh, local fruits and veggies when we are bundled in our winter coats and boots.

The best way to keep track of what's in season is to print off an availability chart for BC-grown fruits and vegetables and tack it up somewhere for easy reference. Look online at farmfolkcityfolk.ca or bcfarmersmarkets.org and see pages 10 to 13 in this book to see what local produce is available each month—both fresh (like lettuce) and stored (like potatoes). Keep in mind that harvests start earlier in the southwest corner of our province, so those in colder climes will have to wait another week or two. Eventually this knowledge will become second nature. An added bonus? Looking forward with anticipation to what's coming next!

EAT SEASONALLY

This is the way we used to eat—savouring everything at its peak. It's best to gorge on vine-ripened tomatoes, fresh sweet corn and perfect peaches while they are plentiful and at their glorious best, and that means in season. Eat enough to ease their absence during the colder months and increase the hankering for next year's harvest. Not only does seasonal eating guarantee best flavour, it offers an ever-changing, diverse parade of fresh fruits and vegetables one after another—nature's plan designed just for us.

FIND LOCAL FOOD SOURCES

Thankfully, this isn't hard. There are many ways to buy locally grown fruits and vegetables. Buying directly from the farmer is best—for us and for them. There are several options:

- Individual farm stands offer perfect opportunities to get local food directly off the field. What could be fresher? Explore rural roads to find these treasures, such as individual farms offering treats like fresh berries or corn at the peak of the season. Larger fruit and vegetable roadside stands often buy produce from several nearby farmers and offer a bigger selection of locally grown foods. Don't pass them by.

- There is something uniquely satisfying about gathering our own food, and U-picks offer the perfect opportunity. Even though we may not be growing them ourselves, we feel a part of the process when we pluck those berries off the bush or cherries off the tree. And it doesn't get any fresher.

- Community-supported agriculture (CSA) boxes, or harvest baskets, are an excellent way to buy a steady supply of seasonal local food straight from the grower. This tradition was started in Japan in the 1970s by a group of mothers who became concerned about imported foods and chemicals used in farming. They contacted several nearby farmers with small plots and asked for weekly harvest boxes with freshly picked vegetables and fruits. They named the project Teikei (loosely translated as "co-operation"), with the slogan "seeing the farmer's face on the food." What a heartwarming concept. Now, CSA boxes have spread across North America, and many BC farms offer this option.

With the CSA program, customers order and pay up front in the spring (or in instalments), providing farmers with a guaranteed income just when they need it to buy seeds and equipment. Weekly CSA boxes with fruits and vegetables harvested the day before are delivered to prearranged pickup spots. Customers can often go directly to the farm as well. Some even provide home delivery. In BC, the average price is between $450 and $550 for fifteen to twenty-two weeks. Boxes can be sized for a couple or family. Produce offerings vary from week to week depending on what's in season and what's ripe in the field. Recipes are often included, especially for unusual veggie surprises. Besides encouraging healthful eating, it's almost like having a labour-free garden in the backyard.

CSA farmers are plentiful around the Lower Mainland and include individual farmers, non-profits and farm schools. But growers all over the province in places like the Fraser Valley, Victoria, Duncan, Nanaimo, Courtenay, the Cowichan Valley, Sechelt, Pemberton, Williams Lake, Smithers, Terrace, Prince George, Nelson, Creston, Vernon, Keremeos, Salmon Arm and Kamloops offer weekly CSA harvest boxes too. Search online or talk to farmers at the local market to find out who they are and what they offer. In many places in BC, it's not hard to put a farmer's face on the fruits and vegetables that end up on the dinner table.

- What's better than strolling through a farmers' market on a sunny morning, coffee in one hand, a basket in the other? Markets offer a wide selection of locally grown foods, harvested the day before, and often the farmer is right there too. Buy lots; buy often. Keep in mind, though, that all markets are not created equal. Farmers' markets that operate only during the growing season (early summer to fall) will most likely sell only locally grown harvests. Markets that stay open all year and have a strict policy of selling local produce exclusively will be overflowing during summer and fall but have meagre offerings—mostly stored root vegetables and apples—during winter and early spring. But many year-round markets sell tourist fruits like bananas and pineapples to fill in the gaps. That makes it hard to know what's local and what isn't. Well-travelled green beans (just like in the grocery store) can appear in January next to local potatoes. Knowing what's in season helps, but buyer, beware: check signs, read the small print and ask questions.

- Finding locally grown produce in grocery stores can be tough. Some produce managers and small grocers make stalwart efforts to buy local fruits and vegetables for their customers. It's important to patronize and encourage those who do, because they deserve it. Pester those who don't so they understand we care.

Roadside stands offer a perfect opportunity to buy fruits and vegetables picked that very morning and to put your food dollars straight into the farmer's pocket. Photo: A. L. Spangler/Shutterstock.com

Don't Start with the Recipe

A generation ago, French housewives used to go to the market in the morning, buy the best-looking produce on offer and decide their menus based on their purchases. The concept is still a good one. Instead of heading off to the grocery store with a list from a chosen recipe, figure out what's in season and then look for a recipe to match. Nowadays, there are countless cookbooks based on seasonal cooking, all beautiful, all inspiring.

KNOW WHERE IT COMES FROM

Today, we want to know everything about the food we eat: nutritional attributes, specific benefits, disease-preventing qualities and best recipes. We research how to eat, following vegan, vegetarian, gluten- or dairy-free, paleo and cleanse diets. We learn about pesticide and fertilizer use and GMO seeds and scrutinize labels. But that's only part of the story. When we buy fruits and vegetables, shouldn't we know where they come from? If we are putting something in our bodies, it makes sense to know where it's been. In the grocery store or year-round markets, that means searching for clues about provenance. Don't be afraid to ask staff to get a clear picture. We deserve to know.

CHOOSE RESTAURANTS CAREFULLY

Many chefs today are local-food fans and buy from nearby farms to offer the freshest fruits and vegetables to their diners. When heading out to eat, reward restaurateurs who believe in serving locally grown food.

PRESERVE THE HARVEST

Always inventive, human beings figured out how to take freshly picked foods from warm summer days and make them last by pickling, fermenting, canning and freezing. So while we can't eat a fresh cucumber in January, we can eat…a pickle. And we won't find fresh BC blueberries or peas in winter, but they freeze beautifully so we can enjoy them in February. BC greenhouse tomatoes are there for us in March, but we can also savour local summer beauties that have been canned in sauce or salsa. Not everyone wants to spend harvest time stirring steaming pots of preserves over a hot stove, but others happily do it for us. Look for enticing jars of jams, pickles, peaches and much more at farmers' markets, prepared from seasonal local produce with love by experts. At home, freezing small batches of produce in season is simple, especially for berries or veggies that need no preparation. A few jars in the pantry and a few bags in the freezer bring summer sunshine into our winter and a sense of satisfaction as well.

Grow Something

Most of us will never be farmers, but even a pot of basil on the windowsill helps connect us to the plants that feed us. Raising a tomato plant on a hot sunny balcony furnishes a sweet, juicy harvest. Growing green onions from bulbs is easy, and rhubarb, planted in a neglected corner of the yard, just keeps on giving. Even sprouting seeds in a Mason jar does wonders for winter salads. Signing up for a community garden plot opens up all sorts of possibilities like growing food from seed. Then, as Wendell Berry writes in his book *Bringing It to the Table: On Farming and Food*, "you will appreciate it fully, having known it all its life."

Make Local Food Social

Savouring a meal around a table with friends and family is one of our great joys. Host a potluck and challenge everyone to bring a dish featuring locally grown fruits or vegetables. Be prepared for ingenious and delicious results, with plenty of interesting conversation. Eating seasonally, the way we used to long ago, brings its own reward, including new and inspiring ways of looking at our food.

Epilogue

Eating is an agricultural act.
—Wendell Berry, *The Pleasures of Eating*

There are times I wish I had been a farmer, rooted in the soil, spending most of my time outdoors. Back to the land and all that. But then I think about how I struggle to grow enough in my vegetable garden to skip the produce section in the summer, and I realize how difficult real farming must be. If I had to rely solely on my efforts—and not the grocery store—to feed my family, we would be decidedly hungry by October.

There's an old saying: if you ate today, thank a farmer. That goes double for those who toil in fields close to where we live. So while BC fruits and vegetables have a starring role in this book, the real heroes of these pages are BC's farmers. Without them, most of us wouldn't have any local food at all.

Their business is a risky one, yet farmers persevere. They face the future—and the weather it brings—with eternal optimism. Adaptability is a must, and hard work is part of the bargain. Expertise is a requirement—gained through farm school, apprenticeships, agricultural degrees, the school of hard knocks or working on the family farm. They care and tend their land with love because they depend on it. They support each other, and they are passionate about what they do.

How fortunate we are that BC farmers continue to labour tirelessly to provide a remarkable cornucopia of foods grown right here where we live—more than enough to satisfy any palate. They deserve our constant encouragement, our economic support and our boundless gratitude.

SUGGESTED READING

GENERAL

Cotler, Amy. *The Locavore Way: Discover and Enjoy the Pleasures of Locally Grown Food.* North Adams, MA: Storey Publishing, 2009.

Edible Vancouver & Wine Country magazine.

Elton, Sarah. *Locavore: From Farmers' Fields to Rooftop Gardens—How Canadians Are Changing the Way We Eat.* Toronto: HarperCollins, 2010.

Goodall, Jane. *Harvest for Hope: A Guide to Mindful Eating.* New York: Warner Books, 2005.

Kingsolver, Barbara. *Animal, Vegetable, Miracle: A Year of Food Life.* Toronto: Harper Perennial, 2008.

Meredith, Leda. *The Locavore's Handbook: The Busy Person's Guide to Eating Local on a Budget.* Guilford, CT: Lyons Press, 2010.

Pollan, Michael. *The Omnivore's Dilemma: A Natural History of Four Meals.* Toronto: Penguin Group, 2006.

Smith, Alisa, and J.B. MacKinnon. *The 100-Mile Diet: A Year of Local Eating.* Toronto: Random House Canada, 2007.

VEGETABLE AND FRUIT GARDENING

Herriot, Carolyn. *The Zero Mile Diet: A Year-Round Guide to Growing Organic Food.* Madeira Park, BC: Harbour Publishing, 2010.

Hole, Lois. *Lois Hole's Vegetable Favourites: A Rich Vegetable Harvest.* Edmonton: Lone Pine Publishing, 1993.

Trail, Gayla. *Grow Great Grub: Organic Food from Small Spaces.* New York: Clarkson Potter, 2010.

Watts, Melanie. *Growing Food in a Short Season: Sustainable, Organic Cold-Climate Gardening.* Madeira Park, BC: Douglas & McIntyre, 2014.

ONLINE RESOURCES

bcfarmersmarket.org BC Association of Farmers' Markets, resource for farmers' markets

bcfarmfresh.com Resource for local food and farmers of the Lower Mainland and Fraser Valley

centralkootenayfood.ca Resource for Central Kootenay food producers, farmers and farmers' markets

circlefarmtour.com Resource for Fraser Valley farm tours

crestonfoodaction.ca Creston Valley Food Action Coalition, resource for farmers' markets and sustainability

eatkamloops.org Resource for Kamloops area farms and farmers' markets

eatlocal.org Vancouver Farmers Markets, resource for Vancouver area farmers' markets

ediblevancouver.com *Edible Vancouver & Wine Country*, magazine promoting local foods in the Lower Mainland, in the Okanagan, and on Vancouver Island

farmfolkcityfolk.ca Farm Folk City Folk, resources for local eating, local foods, BC farmers, events, sustainability

gokootenays.com/farmers-markets Resource for Kootenay farmers' markets

greentable.net/home/farmers-markets Resource for farmers' markets around Vancouver, the Okanagan, Cariboo and Interior, Vancouver Island and northern BC

huafoundation.org/thechoiproject Resource for local Chinese vegetables

islandfarmfresh.com Resource for Vancouver Island farms and farmers' markets

weheartlocalbc.ca Resource for BC farmers and local foods

HEIRLOOM
TOMATOES
$3.50/lb.

Photo: Dane Dreaner/Unsplash

INDEX

Photo: Christina Prinn/Istock

AUTHOR BIO

PHOTO: MONIQUE DE ST. CROIX, UNIQUE PERSPECTIVES

After spending her childhood in colder and more remote parts of Canada, Jane Reid ended up in balmy Vancouver as a young adult. For the past twenty-five years, Jane has lived in Whistler with her husband, raised three children and worked as a community pharmacist. She spends her time writing, gardening, volunteering and enjoying the outdoor pursuits the area has to offer. This book, her first, enabled her to combine her love of the written word with her passion for locally grown foods.